"In your church, does the fire of the Easter season begin and end with Easter Sunday? Does your commemoration of the Easter season lead only to Christ's death and resurrection, and reach no further beyond?

"Although this book was written mainly for Catholics, it provides persons of all denominations with practical, Scripture-based suggestions for celebration and worship experiences from Easter Sunday to Pentecost."

The Joyful Noiseletter

"*Easter for 50 Days* is a how-to manual for celebrating the Easter season. Though it was written for parish planners, the manual provides numerous activities and suggestions for Bible reflection that families and adults can adapt and use at home to celebrate the weeks after Easter."

Faith Today

"This new 'how-to' manual highlights the planning of parish-wide celebrations during this liturgical season and shows how the combined 90 days of Lent-Paschal time offer a community the opportunity 'to listen to the stories and to live the great mysteries of redemption.' The authors share their tried ideas for liturgical celebrations that will 'renew, inspire, and revitalize parish awareness of the unique promise of Paschal time.' This will be a resource useful for those involved in RCIA work. It is particularly recommended by the North American Forum on the Catechumenate as offering a vision and practical suggestions for mystagogy."

Caravan

"For those who believe in the Lord, all things come in due season. For those who believe in the Rite of Christian Initiation of Adults, this book fills a gap that has existed in most parish RCIA programs, namely, the mystagogy section. We have celebrated the rite for the 40 days of Lent. Now we are called to complete the whole 90 days of initiation with 50 days of feasting.

"This book describes the way to do it. It is for not only the catechumens and candidates and their sponsors, but the whole church. This is an important book, helping us discover how to do such feasting clear through Pentecost!"

Modern Liturgy

"Three authors have brought together their collective experience in the RCIA to address the perennial post-Easter-Vigil challenge: how to stretch the church's Easter season of joy over fifty days and, concurrently, how to observe the period of mystagogy. Beginning with some introductory summary statements concerning the RCIA and the Easter season, the authors quickly move on to provide reflections on the Easter Scriptures, activities for children, suggestions for parish organizations, and even a format for an RCIA 'reunion' retreat. The book is literally packed with practical material for the season."

Pastoral Music

"This book is intended for parish leaders who prepare for the season within the context of the parish at large, not just for those who lead the neophytes. It presents ways in which this sacred season can be explored, and addresses all who celebrate it in faith: the adult parishioner, the neophyte, and parish children. Its design proclaims 'Let us as a parish celebrate Eastertime!'"

Newsletter of the North American Forum on the Catechumenate

Easter for 50 Days

Bernard J. Maxwell, Judy Foster, & Jill Shirvington

Foreword by James B. Dunning

88866

TWENTY-THIRD PUBLICATIONS
Mystic, Connecticut

Second printing 1990

North American Edition 1989
Twenty-Third Publications
185 Willow Street
P.O. Box 180
Mystic, CT 06355
(203) 536-2611

Originally published by Desbooks
56 Wales Street, Thornbury 3071,
Victoria, Australia

© Copyright 1989 Bernard J. Maxwell, Judy Foster, Jill Shirvington.
All rights reserved. No part of this publication (with the exception
of banner and vestment designs, and activity sheets to be used in class)
may be reproduced in any manner without prior written permission of
the publisher. Write to Permissions Editor.

ISBN 0-89622-367-1
Library of Congress Catalog Card Number 88-51302

Foreword

Catholics should know how to throw parties. We are a sacramental church with smells and bells that eagerly searches for ways to celebrate life with seven sacraments and 70 x 7 sacramentals. Hilaire Belloc insists:

> Where e're the Catholic sun doth shine
> There's music and laughter and good red wine.
> At least I've heard them tell it so,
> "Benedicamus Domino."

Why is it, then, that mystagogy, the 50 days of Easter when our new members are invited to savor the mysteries of Jesus' dying and rising, is a disaster in many parishes?

Some claim RCIA ministers and neophytes are exhausted after Easter with no energy to celebrate. Others suggest that North Americans see the RCIA like a school calendar with Easter as graduation. A survey reveals that 85 percent of Catholics state that the main purpose of baptism is forgiveness of original sin, not a calling to celebration and mission. If Catholics communicate that to neophytes, no wonder they disappear after Easter.

Others insist that everything closes down during April-May, that parishes are gearing up for June graduations, weddings, and spring weekends at the beach. When I was in Australia and New Zealand, the home of the authors of this fine volume, I learned that neophytes there pulled the same disappearing act, even though it is autumn leading into winter.

Part of our response should be to take seriously *The Rite of Christian Initiation of Adults* (para. 75), the section on the catechumenate period. There the rite insists that exposure to and involvement in mission and witness is part of the catechesis of that period. Mission should not come as a surprise after Easter. Also, catechumens should be informed before Easter that our bishops take mystagogy so seriously that they ask for monthly meetings for a year after initiation in order to deepen their conversion and support them in their baptismal mission. Neophytes find that the church they experienced in a small catechumenal community is not matched by the church of huge crowds that they experience after initiation. They need a small community for support.

The compelling vision and practical suggestions of *Easter for Fifty Days* are another response to mystagogical malaise. The authors are especially wise to take seriously what the RCIA says about this period: *The* catechesis during mystagogy is the Easter eucharists. There, with homily and perhaps catechesis after Mass, neophytes continue to reflect upon God's Word and hear especially what the Acts of the Apostles and the Gospel of John reveal about baptismal vocation. There they might also witness to the parish by telling what Easter, initiation, and mission mean to them and invite old Catholics into the enthusiasm of new Catholics. There they turn from fasting to feasting, they experience parties, and they celebrate with joy what God is doing in their lives.

Kudos to our friends from "down under" for adapting this important and practical volume for us North Americans, and for inviting us to savor the "music, laughter, and good red wine."

James B. Dunning
President, North American Forum on the Catechumenate

Contents

Foreword   *v*

1

Celebrating Easter for Fifty Days!   13

Fasting and Feasting   13
The Way It Was   13
Easter in the Scriptual Tradition   14
The Cycle of Our Lives   14
The Church's Cycle of Life   14
A Community Experiencing Easter Through Adult Initiation (R.C.I.A.)   15
The Catechumenate: Journey of Faith   16

2

Reflecting on the Easter Scriptures   19

The Word of God   19
The Emmaus Event   20
The Sunday Gospels of Paschal Time   20
Waves, Waves: Banners for Lent to Pentecost   21
Sunday Gospels—Easter to Pentecost   22
Reflecting on the Sunday Scriptures   24
The Daily Readings of Paschal Time   26

3

Celebrating Easter with New Christians (Mystagogia)   29

The New Planting   29
What Kind of Community?   30
The Fifty Days   31
"Mystagogia"   31
Ministry   33
The Sunday Masses of the Easter Season   33
The Lectionary and Catechesis   34
Pentecost Is Mission Sunday   35

4

Easter-Pentecost in the School — 39

The Facts — 39
A New Look at Easter Time — 40
Paraliturgy after Easter Vacation — 41
Children's Liturgy of the World—Easter to Pentecost — 42
Celebrating the Sunday Gospel with Children — 43
Children's Activity: Symbols—Year A — 44
Children's Activity: Symbols—Year B — 46
Children's Activity: Symbols—Year C — 48
Paraliturgy to Welcome Ordinary Time — 50
Follow-up Activities — 52
Easter Activities Checklist — 53

5

Your Parish—An Easter Parish — 55

An Easter People — 55
Why an Easter People? — 56
The Catechumenate — 56
Making Your Parish Church an Easter Church — 57
Sign and Symbol — 59
Contemporary Symbols — 59
The Frontispiece — 60
An Easter People Commissioned — 61
Celebrating Easter as a Family — 61
Parish Checklist — 65

6

Liturgical Visuals — 67

The Liturgy Group — 67
Design Procedure — 67
Banners — 68
Method for Transferring Design and Making Banners — 69

The Vertical Banner	70
The Horizontal Banner	72
Audiovisuals	72
3-D Displays	73
Easter 3-D Display Suggestions	74
Ascension	74
Pentecost	74
Dance and Drama	75

7

The Easter Journey—Implications 77

Plan for 90—Not 40!	77
A New Look at the "Basic" Sacraments	78
Baptism	79
Confirmation	81
Eucharist	83
Reconciliation—for an Easter People	85
Panels for the Sacraments of Initiation and Reconciliation	86
Symbols	87
An Alternative Reconciliation Banner	88
The Catechumenate Concludes	89
Annual Retreat—Reunion—Twilight Retreat	90
Session 1: Remember Yesterday	90
Session 2: Dream About Tomorrow	91
Session 3: But Live Today	91

Suggested Resources List 93

1

Celebrating Easter for Fifty Days!

Fasting and Feasting
Most Christians would agree that we are better at fasting for forty days (Lent) than feasting for fifty (celebrating Easter). Lenten traditions of doing penance have dominated our church practice. In reality, Lent was a time of preparation for celebrating new life at Easter...and this for fifty days!

We invest our energies in lenten programs leading to the Easter sacraments and then, it's all over. Apart from our celebration of Holy Week, Easter is likely to be a non-event. Are we the victims of lenten "overkill"? Do we find the whole idea of "feasting" for fifty days "uneasy"?

The Way It Was
The resurrection of Jesus was the first celebration of the early Christian communities. Sunday by Sunday, they relived the presence of the risen Lord in their assembly. These early communities easily adapted the Jewish liturgical cycle of Exodus/Passover to their understanding of the death/resurrection of Jesus and the coming of the Spirit.

The vitality of the early communities flowed from their preoccupation with the Easter event. The development of Paschal time (Easter to Pentecost) was the most natural outcome of a community's reflecting on its emerging traditions.

But, how can we make Easter central in the life of our communities?

Easter in the Scriptural Tradition

The Lukan writings (third gospel and Acts of the Apostles) helped form the time sequence by which the early communities celebrated Easter. Luke outlines the forty days of resurrection and a further ten days from Ascension to Pentecost, and this determined the pattern of the fifty days of Easter.

As well as using this Lukan time sequence, communities began to draw upon the fourth gospel (John) as the source of their reflections on the risen Lord. Thus, by the end of the fourth century a trilogy of Christian Scriptures was integral to the celebration of the Easter-Pentecost cycle.

The Cycle of Our Lives

As members of the human family, we are touched by two distinct experiences of time. On one level, we see our life starting with birth and moving toward death, following some kind of time line. This is called linear time.

At another level, we experience recurring patterns: our year follows a cycle of three hundred and sixty-five days. Birthdays come and go, anniversaries are celebrated, one season succeeds another. We enter grade school, move on toward high school, then possibly college education—always new beginnings.

Then there are the profound experiences of life and death observed in nature and encountered in our own personal lives. This is known as cyclic time. Its purpose is:

- to recall memories;
- to look back at the past and discern patterns;
- to relive joys, sorrows, and momentous decisions;
- to reassess life's direction and values;
- to give continuity to our lives, connecting past and future;
- to grow in wisdom as we learn from our experiences.

Above all, cyclic time puts us in touch with the deeper mysteries of life. As we look back down the spiral of our life, we see there is death and sorrow as well as joy and new life. It takes time to ponder and celebrate these great mysteries.

The Church's Cycle of Life

The arrangement of feasts and seasons that we call the liturgical or church year is based on this concept of cyclic time.

The church of the fourth century, "liberated" under Constantine, found itself immersed in Graeco-Roman culture and society. This culture and society moved within a well-established framework of pagan festivals and celebrations, more often than not related to the seasonal cycle.

Through adapting some of these, Christian communities began to establish a pattern of celebrating the main events in the life of Jesus. More importantly, the celebration of the Lord's resurrection took on a new significance. Always the weekly focus of the community assembling and breaking word and bread, it now underwent a development that had far-reaching implications. Initiation into the Christian community, into the dying and rising of Jesus, emerged as that once-a-year celebration that gathered up all members of the community for forty days of preparation and reflection. Then, through word and sacrament, sign and symbol, new members were "born" to proclaim the goodness and mercy of a loving God—and this for fifty days. The profound effect that this had on a community could only be gauged by the sincerity and vitality of their celebrations.

Nowadays the church proposes a calendar of festivals so that each year Christians have the opportunity to reflect upon and "remember" the great mysteries of their faith. We are thus led through a sequence of sacred events: the Incarnation (Advent-Epiphany), the death-resurrection-ascension of Jesus (the Paschal mystery—[Lent-Easter]) to the coming of the promised Spirit (Pentecost).

These cyclic celebrations are rather like the rings of the trunk of a great tree or spirals on a shell. Through them we are drawn into ever deepening circles of experience. In moving from death to life, from sorrow to joy, from despair to hope, we live the Paschal (Easter) event in our own lives. Thus, life and worship interconnect.

The most significant time in the church's year is the fifty days of the Easter season. Is this reflected in our parish calendars? Are we not more "at home" with the penitential spirit of Lent than celebrating the joy and new life of Easter? To become an Easter people is surely one of the challenges of *being* church today.

A Community Experiencing Easter Through Adult Initiation (R.C.I.A.)
A parish community has welcomed a group of new Christians at the Easter Vigil. It was an unforgettable experience. Their journey of faith had been long. Life stories were shared, minds and hearts were opened to the Good News, life patterns and decisions discerned in the light of the gospel. And then the Easter

sacraments were received. The Vigil took on its full meaning: a life-giving experience for all present. These "new ones" had experienced the process and rites of a special journey: the catechumenate.

The new members of the parish had followed through four stages of a special journey.

> **The Catechumenate: Journey of Faith**
>
> People entering the first period of the catechumenate are called Inquirers. They share life stories and ask life questions. They move to the next period through the celebration of a Rite of Welcome.
>
> In this second period they are known as catechumens. It is a time when the minds and hearts of the catechumens are opened to the Good News of Jesus Christ and they begin to experience a living church, in which they are called to discipleship and *mission*.* A Rite of Election seals this period and opens the way to the next.
>
> The third part of the catechumenate period parallels the forty days of Lent. The catechumens are now recognized as those elect or chosen for the Easter sacraments of baptism, confirmation, and eucharist. This is a time of healing and strengthening as lifestyles are examined against key gospel stories.
>
> This third period culminates in the Rite of Initiation, the Easter sacraments by which the elect pass through the saving waters, are anointed with the sacred oil, and receive the bread of life.
>
> The final and fourth period—mystagogia—spans the fifty days of Paschaltide.* The new Christian or neophyte is drawn more fully into the ministries and *mission* of the community while pondering the great mysteries experienced at initiation.

But questions arise:

1. Can the community continue to adequately support its new members?
2. What lasting impact does the presence of these new members have on the community?
3. Has the faith journey of the new members now ended or is it only just beginning?

In the early Christian communities, the initiation of new members really highlighted what Easter was about. Here was celebrated:

- their passage from death to new life—their personal exodus,
- their acceptance of Jesus, the risen Lord, as their savior.

* In the United States, the duration of both the catechumenate and mystagogia has been extended. See *Rite of Christian Initiation of Adults*, Appendix III, National Statutes for the Catechumenate, 6 and 24.

In the fifty days that followed, the new Christians opened up their lives to the mysteries of life and faith, and the community walked with them. It had an amazing effect. The new Christians entered into a closer relationship with the community; the Easter Scriptures assumed a new meaning; the community was renewed by the presence and enthusiasm of its new members.

This was the time for exuberance, for feasting, for rejoicing, for extravagance: the "Alleluias" were not only sung, but lived!

There is little doubt that this same spirit can touch all parishes that have a catechumenate. The presence of new Christians is a tremendous sign of God's giftedness and hope for the future. They can even startle us out of our complacency!

In the mind of the church, the catechumenate offers a renewed approach to the celebration of Easter and Paschaltide. Where we fail to grasp this, the spiritual vitality of a community is impaired.

The catechumenate is the normative way through which adults come to faith within our Christian community. Beginning when the young church was struggling to survive, a process germinated, took root, and blossomed through rites (*liturgia*), ministry (*diakonia*), and the handing on of the Good News of Jesus Christ (*kerygma*), within the fellowship of community (*koinonia*). Its restoration flowing from the Second Vatican Council is only now being perceived for what it really is. It is not just an academic revival of the theology of the sacraments of initiation. Rather, its potential and far-reaching effects are now seen as a major contribution to the church's pastoral mission of evangelization. It is not a renewal program, yet a community that wholeheartedly opens its life to the rites and process of the catechumenate cannot help but be renewed.

The order of the catechumenate is outlined in the *Rite of Christian Initiation of Adults*. It has been described as a radical document because it challenges all to realize what it means to be a Christian community, a community on *mission*, for the goal of Christian initiation is mission. This document is referred to as the R.C.I.A.

R.C.I.A. develops certain key concepts:

Community: A person comes to faith *within the Christian community*. It is the community's responsibility to welcome and walk with inquirers, to discern their readiness, and to support them throughout their lifelong journey of faith.

Ministry: This essential factor in the journey of faith calls forth the gifts and talents of the community. It is exercised through hospitality, faith sharing, catechesis, prayer support, sponsorship/walking with, etc.

Lectionary-Based Catechesis: Here is found the core material not only for weekly catechesis but also for ongoing formation. The Lectionary presents an exposition of the Christian story proclaimed in the context of community assembled for worship and mission.

Process: The journey of coming to faith is divided into four periods:

1. Precatechumenate: a time of initial questions and shared life stories.
2. Catechumenate: a time of faith formation and service.
3. Election: a time of strengthening and healing through prayerful reflection on the Word of God during the great community retreat—Lent.
4. Mystagogia: a time of deepening baptismal commitment supported by ministry and flowing into mission—the great Pentecost—Paschaltide—the fifty days.

Rites: These four periods are linked by rites or stages, celebrating the completion of one period and being welcomed into the next. The rites are not superfluous but essential components of the overall process of coming to faith.

Companionship/Sponsorship: The responsibility of supporting and walking with the candidate/neophyte throughout his or her lifelong journey of faith can no longer be taken lightly. The sponsor/companion is the "community" person.

Mission: This challenge is extended to the entire parish community, for to live and act as disciples-witnesses of the risen Christ applies equally to all, and calls all to mission.

The process of conversion is incomplete unless the time of mystagogia (the fifty days) is taken seriously. As in the early church, it is within the community that the risen Christ is found, that we come to Easter faith.

2

Reflecting on the Easter Scriptures

The Word of God

Scripture, the Word of God, has that incredible capacity to touch our lives. If we dare to listen, our hearts can be opened to new possibilities. We see the journey of our life in a new context. Gospel values seep into the very fabric of life.

The context for proclaiming the Word of God is within the community. We journey as a community of believers. Together, we "break open" the Word that

- probes and reveals
- challenges and demands
- consoles and sustains
- offers life and hope.

God has not ceased to address his pilgrim people!

The Scriptures of Easter time reveal the presence of the risen Lord to his community. The disciples of Jesus, faced with the events of passion and death, found their meaning in the light of his resurrection. The Paschal event of dying/rising was perceived as a pattern for Christian living. We, too, can enter into this Paschal mystery and verify its meaning in our life journey. This is the thrust of the fifty days of Easter.

The Emmaus Event

The Paschaltide lectionary contains one of the most challenging of the post-resurrection stories—the Emmaus "journey." A charismatic popular leader is executed. Jealousy, politics, and betrayal all play their part. Family, friends, and followers are shattered. Dead heroes were no new phenomenon in the Middle East of Jesus' day (Acts 5:36-37). But this Galilean preacher was different; he rose from the dead, perhaps for some destroying his own credibility (Acts 17:32 and Acts 23:8). The empty tomb would always prove a problem. His disciples began to abandon the movement.

Two of them walk away from this community in turmoil. Yet, although their expectations have been totally destroyed something still remains. They are despondent and yet impelled to discuss the events that have triggered off their decision to get away from it all. First, they were confronted by the cross and now this rumor of an empty tomb. Then they are joined by a stranger who walks with them—Jesus, the mystagogue! He accepts them as they are and, using Scripture and story and tradition, he opens their minds and their hearts. Yet it is only "at table" that they come to recognize him, know him again in the "breaking of the bread."

The reaction when their eyes are "opened" is classic. They turn around (*metanoia*—conversion) and head back to the community to tell their story. The community restates its position first: the Lord is risen! Two stories, that of the women and now this of the two disciples, coincide and Jesus stands among them. Unlike the doubting disciple of the fourth Gospel, Luke's two

disciples make no personal profession of faith. Their hearts, though, are now on fire. And it is to the community they return to authenticate what they have "seen" and believed.

The Scriptures of the Paschal lectionary are not intended as treatises proving the resurrection of Jesus. They are the recorded memories of the first Christian communities pulsating to the rhythm of living faith. For two thousand years they have touched the hearts and imaginations of all Christians. Thus, the liturgical celebrations of Easter aim to "plant" that Word in the hearts of all who follow Jesus. Hearts are meant to "burn" in the process of coming to faith; the whole person is affected; Jesus transforms lives.

The Sunday Gospels of Paschal Time

The Gospel readings of Paschal time emphasize the presence of the risen Lord in the community. Although Year A is the preferred cycle of readings for the catechumenate, those of Years B and C can also be used, as:

- the 2nd Sunday of Easter has the same gospel reading for years A, B, and C: John 20:19-31.
- the 3rd Sunday of Easter in each cycle is centered around specific locations: Emmaus (Year A), Luke 24:13-35; Jerusalem (Year B), Luke 24:35-38; Galilee (Year C), John 21:1-19. Hence, wherever the disciples of Jesus are, he is not far from them.
- the 4th Sunday of Easter drawing on John 10 reflects on the risen Lord as not only "Gate" of the Sheepfold, but also the Good and True Shepherd. Year A, John 10:1-10; Year B, John 10:11-18; Year C, John 10:27-30.
- the 5th and 6th Sundays of Easter are from the last discourse of Jesus at the Paschal supper, rich in thought-provoking imagery for new Christians:
  5th Sunday: Year A, John 14:1-12; Year B, John 15:1-8; Year C, John 13:31-35.
  6th Sunday: Year A, John 14:15-21; Year B, John 15:9-17; Year C, John 14:23-29.
- the 7th Sunday of Easter, presenting the high priestly prayer of Jesus, forms a continuous text from John 17 for Years A, B, and C. Year A, John 17:1-11; Year B, John 17:11-19; Year C, John 17:20-26.

If Paschal time is to be taken seriously, then parish teams will need to discuss and plan their liturgy and visuals well in advance of the Easter season.

The following tables are included to enable teams to view Paschal time in its entirety and to offer some direction for planning. They are also designed to be used in conjunction with the "Waves, Waves" banner shown below and in full color on the back cover. Banners and readings for Ascension and Pentecost are also included. Ascension, though a weekday celebration, is important in the plan of the Paschal mystery. Pentecost, with its vigil and daytime readings, is a veritable treasure house of Scripture, poetry, and visual imagery. These are marvelous resources for reflection for any Easter community.

Waves, Waves: Banners for Lent to Pentecost
The wave design of the ninety days from Lent to Pentecost is based on the idea of the cyclic time of the liturgical year. A stone is thrown into a pool and waves radiate from the center: the risen Lord.

As one part of life ends, another begins. There is always time for change and growth. The colors change from dark somber tones of Lent to the bright festive new life colors of Easter time and Pentecost—a movement from darkness to light (see chart on pages 22-23).

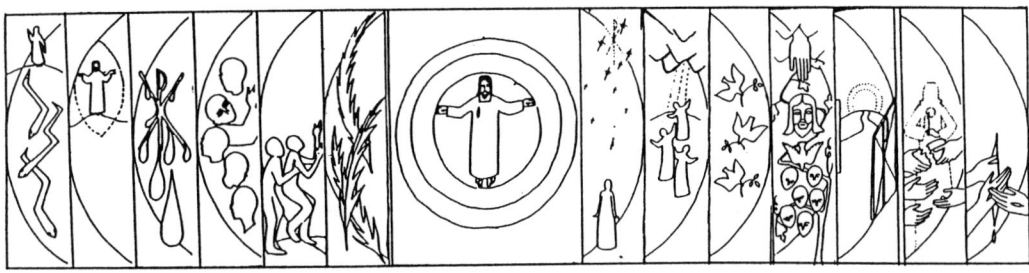

Sunday Gospels   Easter–Pentecost

Reflection		Symbols	Colors
Easter Suday Year A...John 20:1-9 Year B...John 20:1-9 Year C...John 20:1-9 He is Risen! Alleluia!		The three circles: night to day aspect of Lent/Easter Figure: the resurrected Christ	First circle: mid-blue Second circle: light blue Third circle: white Figure: white robe, beige skin, black hair, red wounds.
Second Suday of Easter Year A...John 20:19-31 Year B...John 20:19-31 Year C...John 20:19-31 The evening of the day of the resurrection—"We have seen the Lord." Eight days later, a wandering disciple encounters the risen Lord in the community—"See these wounds"..."My Lord and my God."		The hand in the wound: represents our doubts. Hands with wounds: Jesus who lovingly holds our doubting hand.	Background: mid-green Our hand: light brown Jesus' hand: white Wounds: red "Wave" line: light green
Third Sunday of Easter Year A...Luke 24:13-35 Year B...Luke 24:25-48 Year C...John 21:1-19 *The Eammaus Journey*—The risen Lord walks with his disciples, unrecognized. "Were our hearts not burning within us...?" *The Jerusalem Discovery*—"He opened their minds." The risen Lord is present in and speaks through his community. *The Galilean Encounter*—"It is the Lord." The risen Lord is present when disciples are fishing and at his word the "catch" is made.		Optional background figure of Jesus: his prescence in Eucharist. Hands breaking bread: our sharing in Eucharist.	Background: light green Figure: yellow Hands: light brown Bread: white "Wave" line: yellow
Fourth Sunday of Easter Year A...John 10:1-10 Year B...John 10:11-18 Year C...John 10:27-30 The risen Lord is the source of life for those who follow him. The risen Lord—the Good Shepherd, a *leader* that differs from those of the "world." (Echoes Ezekiel 34:15-16.) The risen Lord *calls* his people to *listen* to his voice and to *follow* him.		Path: the Way we must go. Gate: Jesus, the Gate through which we must pass. "Sun": heaven	Background: acid green (yellow green) Path: light brown Gate: white; red chi-rho Sun: deep yellow "Wave" line: white
Fifth Sunday of Easter Year A...John 14:1-12 Year B...John 15:1-8 Year C...John 13:31-35 The risen Lord answers two questions for his disciples—"How can we know the way? How can we see God?" The risen Lord is the *true vine* linking God and his chosen ones—"Remain in me." The risen Lord *tells* how his disciples will be known,		Hand in clouds: God the Father Face: Jesus the Son Dove: Holy Spirit Small faces: us	Background: deep yellow Hand: green Face: beige Dove: white Our faces: shades of light brown, fawn, yellow "Wave" line: orange-yellow

Reflection		Symbols	Colors
Sixth Suday of Easter Year A...John 14:15-21 Year B...John 15:9-17 Year C...John 14:23-29	The risen Lord's *promise*—the gift of the Spirit. The risen Lord's *request* of the friends he has chosen. The risen Lord's *gift*—his peace is the guarantee of his presence.	Birds: we are all to be "doves of peace"	Background: orange-yellow Birds: white Leaves: green "Wave" line: orange-red
Feast of Ascension Year A...Matthew 28:16-20 Year B...Mark 16:15-20 Year C...Luke 24:46-53	Now no longer room for doubt..."*I am with you.*" The risen Lord continues to work through his friends: "*Proclaim the Good News.*" The parting message of the risen Lord: "*You are my witnesses.*"	Ascension Hand in clouds: God Figures: we, the community Rays of light: path of Ascension	Background: deep orange Clouds: white Hand: green Figures: shades of green
Seventh Sunday of Easter Year A...John 17:1-11 Year B...John 17:11-19 Year C...John 17:20-26	The risen Lord *prays for his friends* who are "*in the world.*" The risen Lord's friends are to be "*in but not of the world.*" The risen Lord prays for *the unity* of all who believe in him.	Figure: represents us as we look in wonder at the heavens of God's creation, a symbol of our resurrection and ascension	Background: orange-red (flame-red) Figure: deep blue-red Stars: metallic gold "Wave" line: metallic gold
Pentecost Year A...John 20:19-23 Year B...John 20:19-23 Year C...John 20:19-23	Pentecost, the day on which the Jewish people recalled the giving of the law on Mount Sinai. For the followers of Jesus, a new day has dawned and a new law is to be preached to all. The gifts are now shared and used for the good of all. The new creation, the breath of the risen Lord..."*he breathed on them: receive the Holy Spirit.*"	Flame of the Spirit and the dove of the Spirit	Background: red Outer circle: mid-blue Inner circle: orange Flame: yellow, or metallic gold Dove: white

Reflecting on the Sunday Scriptures
The following reflections are designed to open up the experience of the Paschal mystery in our own lives and to challenge us to look at ourselves as Easter communities. We gain much from the ongoing support of a group striving to discover the risen Lord in their midst and trying to make sense of the death-resurrection experience of Jesus in their own lives. Let's be careful lest we center upon a purely personal experience of the risen Lord; as communities looking toward the year 2000, we need to keep alive the memory of Jesus, we need to sustain a joyful enthusiasm, we need to recover that desire to spread the Good News.

The first questions are more personally reflective, the final question(s) usually centers upon some aspect of our community's response. They are merely "starters": catechumenal teams or group leaders are expected to adapt and build upon these questions in the light of the needs of their group. In parishes where there is no catechumenate, home gatherings for interested parishioners are encouraged.

Easter Sunday
- Have I experienced life arising out of death?
- When do I find myself disbelieving?
- Why do Christians still believe?

Second Sunday of Easter
- Think of a time when you were like Thomas. What was your doubt?
- How did you come to believe?
- "Peace be with you"; what are the obstacles to peace in your life?
- It is said "seeing is believing." Do you find this so in your own Christian living?
- Is the model of community, described in Acts 2:42-47 ideal, or unreal? In what sense can we be Christian communities today? What is you hope for this parish community?

Third Sunday of Easter
- Reflect back on your own Emmaus journey. What was your "loss"? Who walked with you?
- How did you come to recognize Jesus in all this?
- Sometimes we have to walk right into the darkness of sorrow and doubt: has this been your experience?
- Why did you choose to do this?
- Is there an alternative?
- How do you recognize Jesus in the breaking of bread in your community?
- Is this difficult sometimes?
- How can our Sunday eucharist be a celebration of the risen Jesus in our midst?

Fourth Sunday of Easter
- When do you long for safe pasture in your life?
- Think of the image of the Good Shepherd; name some feelings about this; think of a time when you needed a good shepherd. Why?
- Do you prefer a twentieth-century image for this gospel?
- In what ways might our community resemble the sheepfold? In what sense are we shepherds for one another?

Fifth Sunday of Easter
- Is there something of Thomas in each of us?
- Talk about this.
- Like Philip, do you long to see just a little more to be satisfied? What do you seek?
- The early Christian communities strove for a balance between the ministries of the Word and prayer and the more practical ministries. Reflect upon your own community and ask what kind of balance it reflects.

Sixth Sunday of Easter
- Have you ever felt "orphaned" in your life?
- How is the Father "with you...and in you"?
- What signs do you recognize that Jesus is living among us as a community?

Ascension
- Have you ever separated from a close friend and then discovered a new way of relating with that person?
- What does Ascension really mean in your life?
- Are we as a community living out the directive of Jesus to "make disciples of all nations"?

Seventh Sunday of Easter
- How do you see yourself as "in the world"?
- What kind of things would you say to your friends in a last letter?
- What do you believe Jesus might say to us as a community today?

Pentecost
- What are your strengths and weaknesses?
- Talk about a person you know who is Spirit-filled.
- All Christians are called to mission: how do we energize the community to accept this mission?

The Daily Readings of Paschal Time

The daily lectionary provides a comprehensive plan of scriptural reflections throughout Paschal time. The continuous reading of the Acts of the Apostles Chapters 4 to 28, coupled with the semi-continuous reading of the Gospel of John, provides a picture of Christian community, both practical and spiritual. Acts describes life in community, the young church in action:

- its fellowship
- its problems and challenges
- its worship
- its living out of the basic gospel
- its great experiences of conversion and healing.

The fourth gospel, "the book of new beginnings," rechallenges the community

- to "see" the signs that Jesus does so that disciples may believe
- to reflect on the triumphant death of Jesus ("If I be lifted up.")
- to probe the meaning of Jesus risen and present wherever disciples are gathered.

The following plan of the extended daily readings of Paschal time is given as a guide for those who wish to use the Paschal Scriptures for sources of prayer and meditation.

WEEK 1
Day	Reading 1	Psalm	Gospel
Monday	Acts 2:14-41	Ps 15	Matthew 28:8-15
Tuesday	2:42-47	Ps 32	John 20:11-18
Wednesday	3:1-26	Ps 104	Luke 24:13-35
Thursday	4:1-22	Ps 8	Luke 24:35-48
Friday	4:21-37	Ps 117	John 21:1-14
Saturday	5:1-16	Ps 117	Mark 16:9-15

WEEK 2
Day	Reading 1	Psalm	Gospel
Monday	Acts 5:17-42	Ps 2	John 3:1-8
Tuesday	6:1-7:1	Ps 92	John 3:7-15
Wednesday	7:2-53	Ps 33	John 3:16-21
Thursday	7:54-8:3	Ps 33	John 3:31-36
Friday	8:4-25	Ps 26	John 6:1-15
Saturday	8:26-40	Ps 32	John 6:16-21

WEEK 3
Day	Reading 1	Psalm	Gospel
Monday	Acts 9:1-19a	Ps 118	John 6:22-29
Tuesday	9:19b-31	Ps 30	John 6:30-35
Wednesday	9:32-43	Ps 65	John 6:35-40
Thursday	10:1-11:18	Ps 65	John 6:44-51
Friday	11:19-30	Ps 116	John 6:52-59
Saturday	12:1-25	Ps 115	John 6:60-69

WEEK 4
Day	Reading 1	Psalm	Gospel
Monday	Acts 13:1-12	Ps 41	John 10:1-21
Tuesday	13:13-52	Ps 86	John 10:22-39
Wednesday	14:1-20	Ps 66	John 12:36-50
Thursday	14:21-28	Ps 88	John 13:16-20
Friday	15:1-12	Ps 2	John 14:1-6
Saturday	15:13-35	Ps 97	John 14:7-16

WEEK 5
Day	Reading 1	Psalm	Gospel
Monday	Acts 15:36-16:10	Ps 113b	John 14:15-24
Tuesday	16:11-40	Ps 144	John 14:25-31
Wednesday	17:1-15	Ps 121	John 15:1-8
Thursday	17:16-34	Ps 95	John 15:9-11
Friday	18:1-23	Ps 56	John 15:12-17
Saturday	18:24-19:7	Ps 99	John 15:18-21

WEEK 6
Day	Reading 1	Psalm	Gospel
Monday	Acts 19:8-20	Ps 149	John 15:26-16:4
Tuesday	19:21-20:6	Ps 137	John 16:5-11
Wednesday	20:6-38	Ps 148	John 16:12-15
ASCENSION	Acts 1:1-11	Ps 46 — Eph. 1:17-23	Luke 24:46-53
Friday	21:1-40	Ps 46	John 16:16-22
Saturday	22:1-29	Ps 46	John 16:23-28

WEEK 7
Day	Reading 1	Psalm	Gospel
Monday	Acts 22:30-23:35	Ps 67	John 16:29-33
Tuesday	24:1-27	Ps 67	John 17:1-11
Wednesday	25:1-27	Ps 67	John 17:11-19
Thursday	26:1-32	Ps 15	John 17:20-26
Friday	27:1-44	Ps 102	John 21:15-19
Saturday	28:1-31	Ps 104	John 21:20-25

From Eugene O'Sullivan O.P., *Readings at Daily Mass*, Catholic Publications Centre, Auckland, New Zealand. Used with permission.

3

Celebrating Easter with New Christians (Mystagogia)

The New Planting

Easter is a vibrant time in parishes with an active catechumenate. New Christians are the greatest gift to any community.

Hundreds of Christian communities throughout the world have carefully nurtured and presented catechumens for the Easter sacraments of initiation. After the great vigil of Easter, they are no longer the chosen catechumens but the community's neophytes, meaning the "new plantings" or "newly planted."* Like all new plantings, care is an essential part of their growth. Each has a unique life of its own; each is meant to grow where it has been planted. But growth depends on certain variables.

If you have ever dabbled in a little gardening, you'll see the connection.

---

* In New Testament Greek, *neophutos* =recently planted—from *neos* (new) and *phuton* (a plant)

Seed beds and boxes are first prepared and then the seeds are sown. Warmth and gentle moisture call the seeds into new life. One begins to watch the miracle of growth. The seedlings bustle each other as they reach up for light and absorb the sustaining energy of the sun. Yet heat and moisture must be regulated. Over-exposure can retard, or even destroy growth. It is a time of care, protection, and watchfulness.

Then the time draws near for the maturing seedling to change its growth pattern. The growth process of the preceding weeks has readied it for independence. Soon it will be moved from its familiar seed-box or bed and join the larger "community" in the world of the garden. Likewise this larger world—the garden—has also been prepared to receive the plant. It has been dug, mulched, and weeded so that the seedling, like the seed of the gospel, may find suitable ground in which to take root. The gardener weighs up the seedlings' chances of survival and these become the "new plantings" in the wider world.

Even then this wider world can have its own snares that inhibit growth: the new plantings must still be cared for and protected until they strike and take root. In catechumenal terms, the garden is the community and the neophyte is the "new planting."

What Kind of Community?

There can be no doubt about the kind of community in which the seed of faith is to be sown and planted. Optimum conditions for that seed to germinate and grow require an atmosphere of interest and welcome, care and love. The periods and stages of the catechumenate are times of preparation and nurturing for both the inquirer and the community. The reflective prayerful period of Lent readies the catechumen for initiation and invites the community to experience again the significance of the Easter sacraments in their lives. The climax is the Easter Vigil, sealing the journey of faith. But, what then?

There are questions to be asked, answers to be given, reflections to be shared. The new Christian needs to sense that he or she belongs to this parish. Eucharist is celebrated together: no longer are they dismissed after the Liturgy of the Word. All now are disciples of the risen Lord, sharing the richness and uniqueness of Christian experience. The emphasis is on community.

Put in practical terms, the community, during this final period of initiation, assumes the role of sponsor. Thus, the community, with the new Christians

- moves forward together
- meditates on the gospel
- shares in the eucharist
- performs works of charity.

The desired outcome of this activity is summarized by the R.C.I.A. document thus: "The community and the neophytes together...grow in deepening their grasp of the Paschal mystery and in making it part of their lives." (R.C.I.A 244 [Latin edition: 37]).

Ideally, then, Paschal time should be the renewal time for the whole community, a time of new growth in the lives of people individually and within groups. Once a community is catechized to grasp this, the new Christians are not only welcomed, but received with great joy, for now we all journey together over these next fifty days.

The Fifty Days
Paschal time can be likened to a great symphony. The predominant melody, the Easter Alleluia, is joyous and enthusiastic, announcing victory over death, the promise of new life, the presence of the risen Lord. These themes resound for a full fifty days.

The score of this Paschal symphony is the message of mystagogia as expressed in the R.C.I.A. It culminates in the great Pentecost crescendo calling all—new Christians and community—to service, to mission, to evangelization. The movements of this symphony can be described as:

- journeying together and sharing gifts
- meditating on the Paschal gospels
- celebrating the eucharist
- serving and witnessing through works of charity
- living in the community of the risen Christ.

These movements are the practical steps proposed by the church for making Paschal time one of renewal for the whole community, and one of joy-filled life for its new members. This is the Spirit imbuing the community of the new Christians.

A community, then, that has seriously walked the journey to Easter reflecting on the Word of God, and supported those preparing for the Easter sacraments of baptism, confirmation, and eucharist finds itself impelled to live the fifty days of Pasch to Pentecost.

"Mystagogia"*
This final period of initiation, "mystagogia," has all the appearances of being a "cinderella" of the catechumenate. We either side-step the issues raised or tend to spend time making up for earlier deficiencies. (That is, anything seen to be omitted during the preceding months of the catechumenate is dealt with now.) The terminology, mystagogia or post-baptismal catechesis, can leave us mystified.

* Confer *Rite of Christian Initiation of Adults*, 244-251.

Of course, there are very good reasons for scaling down our involvement with the catechumenate after Easter: there is a welcome Easter break; the hard work an active parish puts into its lenten programs and preparation for Easter necessitates taking that Easter holiday; the physical and emotional strain experienced by an initiating community is felt once the Vigil is over.

But mystagogia is still a time of initiation, of ongoing formation and conversion. The fifty days of Paschal time must not be divorced from the forty days of Lent. The essential priorities of mystagogia are ministry, witness, and mission. Indeed, mystagogia challenges a community to reflect and question its commitment to these priorities. Likewise, the "quality" of a catechumenate can be discerned from the way it understands and lives mystagogia.

The R.C.I.A. emphasizes the following:
1. The lectionary of Paschal time (for both the Sunday and weekday readings) forms the basis for post-baptismal catechesis.
2. The neophytes' new personal experience of the sacraments and of the community are the power bases of this time of initiation.
3. The Easter gospels bring a new dimension to the neophytes' understanding of the mysteries of death and resurrection, experienced in their own lives (Romans 6:8-11).
4. Post-baptismal catechesis aims to help the neophyte reach a new sense of faith, the church, the world.
5. The neophytes experience a renewal of mind and heart, discovering the goodness of the Lord and sharing in the Holy Spirit (R.C.I.A., 245 [Latin edition, 38]).

Mystagogia is also a time for listening to stories, but this time the stories are of our new Christians. Just as the catechumenate team encouraged the inquirers to tell their stories during the pre-catechumenate, mystagogia deals with stories again—stories of the new disciples who have met their risen Lord. They have experienced the mystery of dying and rising, of victory over death. They have come from their encounter and, like the two disciples on the road to Emmaus, they now hasten back to the community, their hearts burning within them, to tell the community the Good News that the Lord has truly risen and walks with them. Stifle this, and post-baptismal catechesis is lifeless!

No package deal or program can successfully bring these experiences to life. Indeed, the great post-resurrectional stories of Scripture, enfleshed in those stories of the neophyte, are the matter of mystagogia. But the neophytes cannot travel alone these last fifty days or tell their stories in isolation. Team and community are indispensable if the mysteries are to be explained, reflected upon, and celebrated. A catechumenal team has much to do during the fifty days of Paschal time: the Emmaus story becomes its model; the Scriptures abound in "material" for reflection and discussion.

Ministry
If mystagogia means trying to make sense of the Paschal mystery in our own lives, then ministry is a natural outcome of this reflection; it is a response to that mystery and living out of one's baptismal commitment. Ministry is the placing of one's gifts at the service of others.

During their formation as catechumens and elect, the neophytes will have seen the community ministering to one another, both in the normal daily events of life and within the context of the liturgy. Thus, ministry is seen to be a normal expression of Christian living.

So one aspect of the post-baptismal catechesis is discerning with the neophytes their own particular gifts and talents and finding opportunities for them to exercise these within the community.* This is an important feature of their formation as it sensitizes the community to the presence of the neophytes and establishes patterns of contact with fellow parishioners.

It is advisable to encourage neophytes to serve initially, in some of the ordinary, everyday "street" ministries (e.g., visiting the sick, helping the elderly, supporting the handicapped, working with core groups). The exercising of liturgical (church) ministries flows much later out of such "street" ministries.

The Sunday Masses of the Easter Season
The R.C.I.A. highlights the significance of the Easter season. Since at the Vigil, the neophytes celebrated a "new, personal experience of the sacraments and of the community," the main setting for the post-baptismal catechesis will be "the so-called Masses for neophytes, that is, the Sunday Masses of the Easter season" (R.C.I.A., 247 [Latin edition, 40]).

These Masses sensitize the community to the presence of new members and challenge the congregation to reflect on their own faith journey. How?

The neophytes are invited to tell the story of their faith journey each Sunday of Easter. The words may not come easily, but their sincerity will be very evident. Gently encourage them to offer this first gift to the community: that

* This process should have commenced during the time of the catechumenate.

Candle designs for Easter

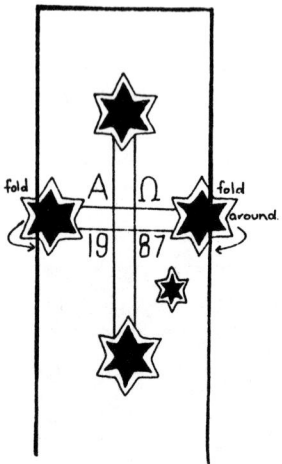

These designs may be made from coloured contact and attached to the candle.

of witnessing to their rebirth in Christ, their rising and their victory with him over death and sin.

Encourage the neophyte to take part in the Sunday eucharist through reading the petitions of the Prayer of the Faithful, or presenting the gifts of bread and wine.

Highlight the symbols of the Easter sacraments. Commence each Sunday eucharist with the blessing and sprinkling of water. Emphasize the procession of the Book of the Gospels with resounding "Alleluias." Let the Paschal candle with its Easter decorations be clearly visible. Give thought to vestments to be worn. Bring out the Easter banners! Adorn the church in such a way that Easter speaks of abundance and festivity and joy. Don't hide the symbols.

The Easter Scriptures should be the basis for all liturgical planning because from here on it is within the Mass that catechesis takes place. Thus, the introductions, penitential rite, the homily, and prayers must reflect the needs of each community.

The Lectionary and Catechesis

It must be emphasized, again and again, that the Sunday lectionary is central to all catechesis throughout the periods of the catechumenate. Scripture touches the lives of individuals, calling them to faith and conversion in a way that preplanned programs simply cannot.

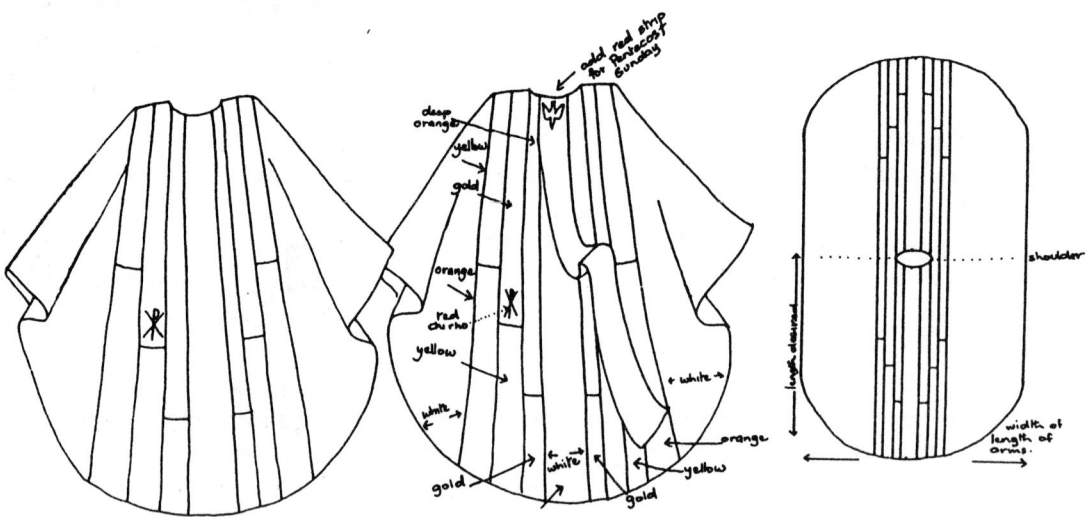

Easter vestments. Use a gold or white stole for Easter time, and a red stole for Pentecost. (see back cover photo)

To ignore the Paschal time lectionary would be to short circuit the ongoing conversion process of mystagogia. The Easter Scriptures speak powerfully of the presence of the risen Lord in the life of the early communities. The catechumenal team should ponder long and carefully the Emmaus event as a model for umystagogia:

- encounter with the risen Lord
- the Scriptures opened and explained
- recognition through the breaking of bread
- the impelling desire to tell the story: mission.

These points have already been explored in Chapter 2.

Pentecost Is Mission Sunday
In the spirit of post-baptismal catechesis, Pentecost is seen less as a finale and more as a celebration of "beginnings." Pentecost, after all, celebrated new beginnings for the first Christian community. It certainly did not bring Easter to a close.

In planning such a celebration of Pentecost, three areas might be kept in perspective:

1. The Emmaus dimension (the revelation of the Lord in Scripture and community) touches the life story of each traveler. Heights have been experienced, questions answered, directions clarified in the light of the Word of God.
2. The community has every reason to celebrate! It has been graced with new life and the challenge of sponsorship.
3. Ministry has been placed in the perspective of service to the community. (If no opportunity for ministry exists, then what does a community offer its new members?)

The celebration of Pentecost should be taken seriously. Each community must develop its own style of celebration, marking this most important "rite of passage" in the life of the new Christians and the community. The whole spirit of the liturgy speaks of readiness for mission and celebrates the power of the Spirit in the lives of disciples.

What are we celebrating?

- For both neophytes and the community, we are celebrating ongoing conversion. Pentecost is a step forward toward a new stage of independence.
- The catechumenate, as such, has come to an end. The neophytes are now guided by the light of the gospel and the support of the wider community.
- It is an opportunity for the neophytes to realize that, from hereon, they identify with the concerns of the community.

- We publicly acknowledge the generosity of the neophytes who, by taking their conversion seriously, wish to live out their baptismal commitment in ministry to the community.
- The entire parish is again missioned for the coming year, to go forth and spread the Good News that Jesus, now risen, is active in the community.

The following suggestions are offered for a lively celebration of Pentecost within a parish community:

1. Inform all parishioners in advance that Pentecost Sunday is to be missioning Sunday for the coming twelve months. Explain the concept that mission is for everyone, not just the ordained and those choosing to help in and around the church. Reflect on the giftedness of each and challenge all to see how their gifts can best be shared with others. After the homily at each Pentecost Mass, parishioners are invited to complete a special Missioning Card. Invite the congregation to bring these up during the presentation of the gifts.

2. After the main Sunday morning eucharist, hold a morning parish get-together with coffee and doughnuts. The new Christians might be encouraged to prepare this as their first act of service in the community that has welcomed them so generously. Alternatively, after the Saturday evening eucharist, a simple basket supper of soup and rolls, might be arranged for the parish—again by the new Christians.

3. Sometime over the Pentecost weekend, there could be a get-together for all who have been part of the catechumenal journey. Pentecost celebrates much more than just casual partings. The journey has been significant for many, and this deserves recognition. It will be an occasion for storytelling, some remembering, prayer and expressions of hope for the future.

4. Give thought to the way Pentecost is to be featured in your community. The signs and symbols of initiation should be evident—the Easter candle suitably adorned, the blessed water for sprinkling. Celebrate the Liturgy of Word and Eucharist with the strong powerful symbols of procession, song, and incense. Plan visual imagery for the occasion: floral arrangements, banners, and special vestments. Surprise the usual Sunday congregation with a warm welcome at the church door!

There is great scope for a parish wishing to highlight the Pentecost event in their parish. Make it a memorable occasion in which the community, along with the new Christians, are both missioned to spread the Good News and committed to the works of the community.

Missioning Card
Pentecost 198...

I,..
a member of St Matthew's Parish, Glenburn, wish to
serve our community by: ....
....
....

(reverse side of card)

'There is a variety of gifts,
but always the same Spirit'.

The community of St Matthew's, Glenburn, welcomes
and accepts your offer of service for this coming year.

....
(President, Parish Pastoral Council)

....
(For the Parish Team)

4

Easter-Pentecost in the School

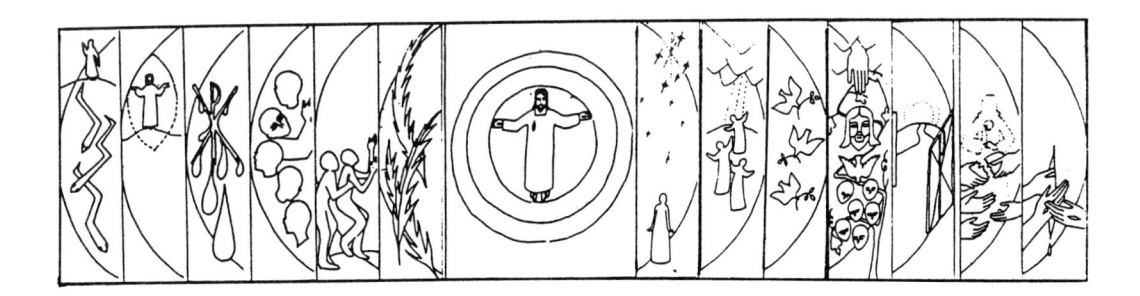

The Facts

As a community, we have become accustomed to the lenten journey of forty days, the solemn days of the Triduum, and the joyous celebrations of Easter Sunday, the climax of the church year. Indeed, it is one of those rare occasions when the church and "society" commemorate the same event, though the mode of celebrating differs vastly.

Catholic schools zealously promote lenten activities, themes, displays, paraliturgies, reflections, sacramental preparation, etc. Holy Week becomes a hive of activity with class groups presenting facets of the Paschal mystery in a variety of ways from Paschal meals to Easter parades! Around 3 P.M. on Holy Thursday, Holy Week becomes holiday time. All too often, religious sentiments are set aside in favor of the Easter break, chocolate eggs and the need to enjoy some relaxation.

Yes, we have become very creative celebrating the forty days of Lent. But, again, what of the fifty days of Easter?

For most, Easter concludes with the Easter Sunday celebrations. It is almost as if the commercial world of consumerism calls the tune, not of joyful Alleluias, but rather of "Let's get on with the buying and selling." Summer is close, and for many, graduation may be the next major event. Besides that, annual vacation is beckoning. Paschal time is really a disjointed time.

Thus its impact is largely lost in many Christian communities today. Yet we are called to turn our creative talents and energies to the celebration of Easter for fifty days. There seems little doubt that we are good at fasting for forty days. But how do we feast for fifty?

A New Look at Easter Time
The Scripture readings of Easter time can put young Christians in touch with the great Easter stories of healing and forgiveness, surprise and adventure.

To implement the spirit of Eastertide, certain areas need close attention. The personnel in each school might pursue this list and order their priorities.

Priority	*Thematic Idea*
Creating a school environment	We are Easter people
Staff inservice	Why celebrate the fifty days of Easter?
Gathering Easter Resources	
Parent Communication	Fasting for Forty; feasting for fifty!
Easter Programs for classes	
Liturgies, paraliturgies, prayer services	Easter...an alleluia event!
Easter in St._____ parish	Welcome the new Catholics
The Paschal lectionary	The risen Jesus is present in his community
Social events	Let everyone rejoice!

The following resources help to open up the the richness of the Easter lectionary for class and Sunday school groups.

Paraliturgy after Easter Vacation

Gathering
Gather the school around a large, beautifully adorned Easter candle. Have the candle already lit.

Introduction
Link the Easter vacation, just enjoyed, with the celebration of Easter Sunday and the remainder of the fifty days (that is why the candle is lit).

Song
"This is the Day" (*Hymnal for Young Christians*). If possible, arrange for percussion, etc.

Prayer
God of our family and friends,
we thank you for the gift of new life:
we feel refreshed by our holiday;
we enjoy the warmth of Easter sunshine;
we see the new life of spring;
we share again life with our teachers
and our friends this term.
Help us to celebrate this gift of life,
the greatest of gifts.
We ask this through Christ our Lord. Amen.

Gospel Procession
The Book of the Gospels, accompanied by lighted candles, is brought forward. The children welcome the Word with an Alleluia song/verse.

Gospel
The story of Easter Sunday morning (John 20:1-9) or the dialogue version from *Lectionary for Masses with Children*, John 20:11-18.

Response
Repeat the Alleluia song.

Talk
Based on the church's invitation to celebrate new life for fifty days until Pentecost. Outline your school's plans for this. Tell the children where the Easter candle is to be placed; make arrangements for flowers to adorn it and someone to light the candle all during Easter time.

Ritual
A class representative comes forward, lights his or her class candle from the Easter candle and leads that class back to their classroom. As they leave, the rest of the school sings, "Light of Christ light our way; light our way as we go" (*Hymnal for Young Christians*).

Children's Liturgy of the Word—Easter to Pentecost
To highlight and enforce the full significance of Paschal time, it is important to offer activities that link what is done in the parish with the home and the local school, and the parish religious education program. The basic "ingredient" for this activity is the Sunday gospel. The format is a symbol based on the gospel, and this is pasted on to a master sheet back in the home.

Schools and catechist classes are invited to spend some time with the gospel on a day either before or after the Sunday celebration. After prayer and song, quiet and sharing, the symbol is presented to each child to take home. A format for this gospel sharing is included in the following pages.

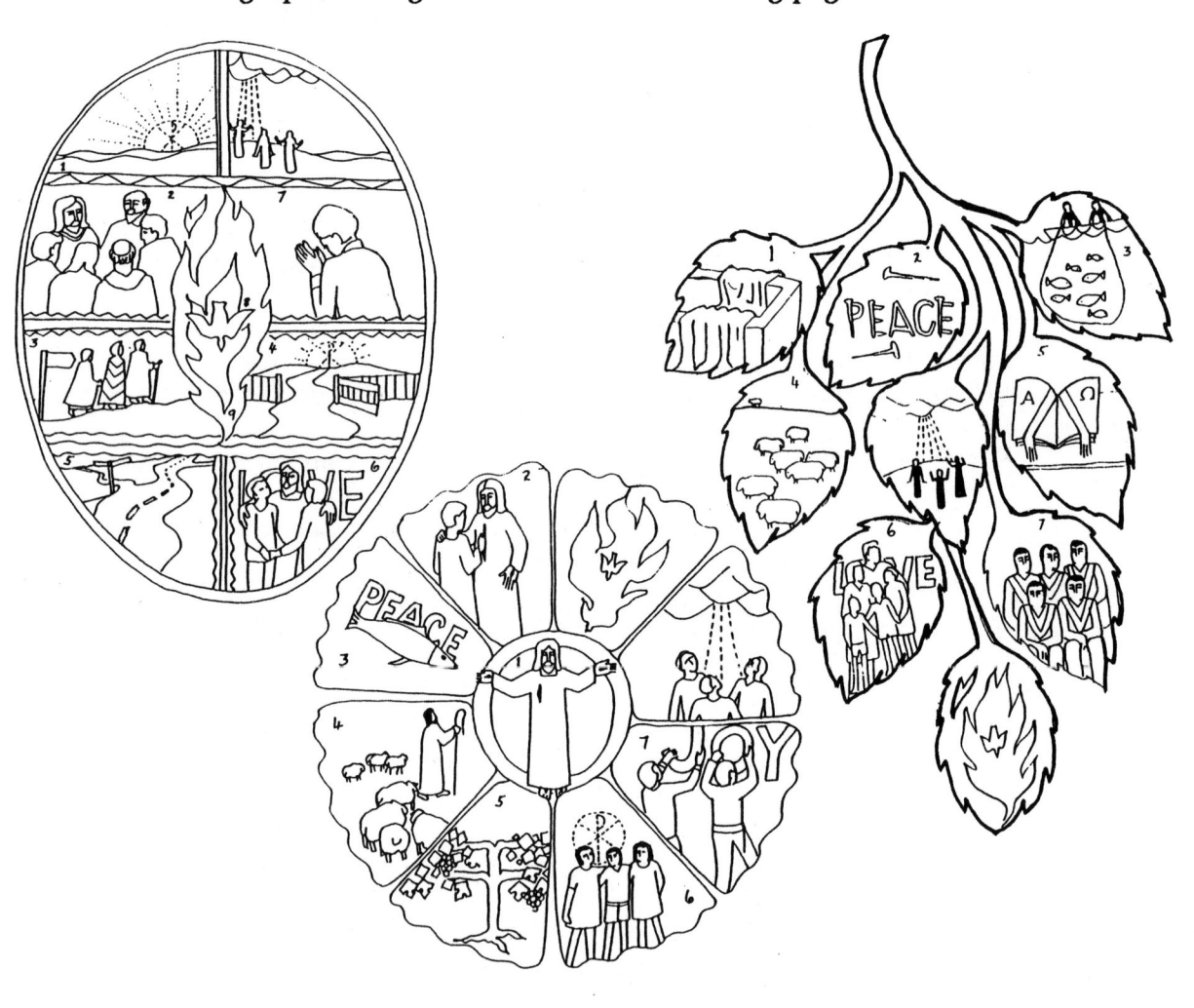

In parishes where children's Liturgy of the Word is celebrated separately from the adults, the children reflect on that gospel together, searching for its meaning in their lives. The symbol is presented at the end of the session. This is pasted on the family poster back at home.

Three different designs are offered in this section. They relate to Years A, B, and C of the lectionary. It is vital that families are well informed of this activity. The distribution of the poster sheet (master sheet) is best done within the Sunday eucharist (e.g., Easter Sunday). However, it may be more convenient for your situation to distribute these before the Easter vacation. The weekly symbols may also be printed separately and published in your parish bulletin.

Celebrating the Sunday Gospel with Children

- Gather around the Table of the Word.
- Pause for a moment to quiet down, to get ready to listen.
- Sing an "Alleluia" song or verse.
- Proclaim the gospel passage for the group. (While older children can understand the lectionary version, younger children do have difficulty. It is suggested that you use the *Lectionary for Masses with Children*, dramatized or dialogue versions or retell the story in your own words.)
- Repeat the "Alleluia" song.
- Share ideas, reflections from the gospel story. Some "starter" ideas for the Easter gospels can be found on the following pages. Strive always to make the discussion life-centered and, where possible, suggest some kind of Christian outreach to others.
- Hand out the appropriate symbol and ensure that the children have made the connection with the gospel of that Sunday.
- Take time for prayer: quiet, intercessory, litany-type, spontaneous, prepared, etc.
- Have a simple dismissal, e.g., "Go in peace, to love and serve the Lord."

Children's Activity: Symbols—Year A

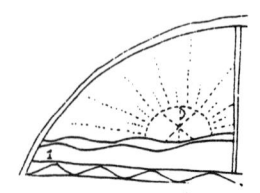

EASTER SUNDAY
Talk about a sunrise you've seen. What did you notice? How did it make you feel? A clear sunrise gives the promise of a clear fine day. A sunrise heralds the end of darkness and stirs up life for this new day. Talk about the events that happened around sunrise the first Easter day.

SECOND SUNDAY OF EASTER
Have you watched a group of people waiting for someone to arrive at an airport or station? Talk about this. What happens when the train arrives, or the plane comes in? The friends of Jesus were gathered together, too, but they couldn't explain their fear, until.... Talk about what happened and the change that took place.

THIRD SUNDAY OF EASTER
Friends often enjoy a walk together, to talk things over, and share ideas. Can you remember a walk like this? The friends of Jesus were sad and puzzled; but a stranger changed all that! What was the surprise?

FOURTH SUNDAY OF EASTER
Being with friends is safe and comfortable. We don't like being separated. Have you ever been lost in a crowd? How did this feel? Talk about the moment when you were found. Today's story tells us about Jesus who wants to care for each one of us. We can't ever be lost to him.

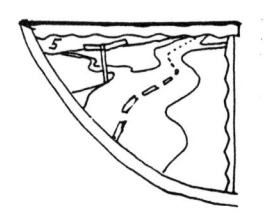

FIFTH SUNDAY OF EASTER
Sometimes a family decides to change houses. Mom and Dad search for the new place; they prepare everything for the move, and then the big day comes. Jesus talks about preparing a place, about life with him. We have no need to worry: Jesus says he is the Way.

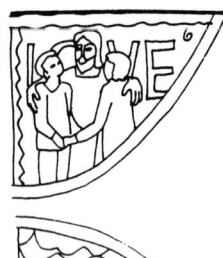

SIXTH SUNDAY OF EASTER
Lots of things in our life follow a pattern. What do you do to get to school each day? How do you spend Easter? Jesus wanted to leave his followers a pattern for living, too. "Love one another" is the clue to happy living.

ASCENSION
Saying "good-bye" is not very easy. We really miss that person who goes away. Can you remember when this happened to you? Yet we somehow know that this person is still part of our life. Jesus cheered his friends: "Know that I am with you."

SEVENTH SUNDAY OF EASTER
Have you ever looked up at a full moon and wondered how many people it was shining down upon, just at that moment? Have you thought who else might be looking at the moon? Maybe you have even bounced messages to others via the moon! Jesus wants us to keep contact with him. So we pray, we talk with him as friend with friend.

PENTECOST
Many people are thinking about peace in our world. Peace groups often use a bird, a dove as the symbol of peace. Can you figure out why (cf. the story of Noah)? The friends of Jesus were living frightened lives; Jesus sent his Spirit of Peace upon them. Talk about what happened in that first Christian community.

Childrens' Activity: Symbols—Year B

EASTER SUNDAY
Unexpected happenings catch people by surprise—everyone talking at once and everyone trying to piece together what really happened. Talk about the first Easter Sunday: the facts (Jesus' body gone, the cloths left) and the mystery (what had happened? where was Jesus?) and his promise (that he would rise again on the third day).

SECOND SUNDAY OF EASTER
Sometimes we find it hard to believe people—for all sorts of reasons. Thomas found it hard to accept that his hero, Jesus, had died. He was slow to believe in this new life of Jesus, but he was helped to get over his doubt and believe. How?

THIRD SUNDAY OF EASTER
Have you ever worked on a jigsaw puzzle and it just wouldn't come out? You try and try and try again. The friends of Jesus were trying to work out the puzzle of Jesus' death and disappearance. Was he truly alive as some disciples said? What do you think after hearing today's gospel?

FOURTH SUNDAY OF EASTER
If you have ever visited a hospital where babies are born, you would notice how precious each baby is: families adore them, each baby has a crib and is named, the sick ones receive special care, etc. That's how it is with Jesus, the Good Shepherd. This story tells of his love and care and concern.

FIFTH SUNDAY OF EASTER
Sometimes we have a big clean up in the garden. It becomes overgrown and bushes need a trim. Have you ever tried to remove a thick, tangling vine? Its long arms grow in all directions, but are connected to the one main root and stem. The vine has great strength. Jesus uses this picture to tell us that's how we belong to him and that it is important to remain connected to the vine.

SIXTH SUNDAY OF EASTER
Friends are one of the most precious gifts we can have. It's hard to imagine how life would be without them. Friendship doesn't come easily—we learn and grow through the friends we have. Jesus gives us a clue about our friendship with him; "Keep my commandments, remain in my love" just like friends, doing things together.

ASCENSION
Have you ever been to the airport to say farewell to someone special? The time comes to say good-bye; we stay to watch the plane race down the runway, and then it disappears from sight. But we do believe that the plane still exists! That person hasn't disappeared. We just can't see far enough. We believe, too, that the presence of Jesus lives on in our lives. The Feast of the Ascension is a celebration of God's time—something we can't understand yet.

SEVENTH SUNDAY OF EASTER
Today's gospel is like a last letter to us from Jesus, before he returns to his Father. He has many thoughtful things to say to us. Most of all though, he wants to give us a share in his joy: "I say these things to share my joy with them, to the full."

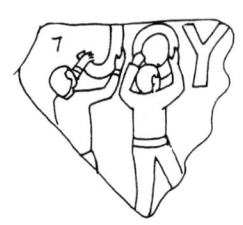

PENTECOST
Lighted candles are an important part of a birthday celebration: we've gathered to celebrate a special person; it's a happy time of being together; there's usually a joyful spirit in the group. The apostles gathered together, too, to help each other decide on what must be done next. Jesus had gone but he had promised to send help, and then the Spirit of life and love and joy was among them.

Children's Activity: Symbols—Year C

EASTER SUNDAY
Have you ever found an empty shell, or a dried-up cocoon, or cicada shell? We wonder what happened to that animal: Did it die? Did it become something different? The life cycles of animals are full of mystery to us. The friends of Jesus came along to care for him, and found an empty tomb, cloths on the ground. What had happened? How could they solve this mystery? Jesus had risen from the dead, as he said he would.

SECOND SUNDAY OF EASTER
Can you think of a time when you were really frightened about something? Then you shared this scary thing with someone close to you; their hug and their words took away the fright, and peace came. That's how it was for Thomas. He was puzzled and confused. He was afraid. Jesus spoke to him, helping him to understand, and peace came.

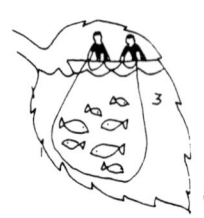

THIRD SUNDAY OF EASTER
Sometimes you have to go out and look for someone in the playground. Because there are so many others around, that person is really hard to find. Then you see their color hair, or the way they bat or run, or some sign that helps you to recognize him or her. The apostles were busy about fishing; this stranger began doing things they recognized—it was a great get-together. Jesus was with them!

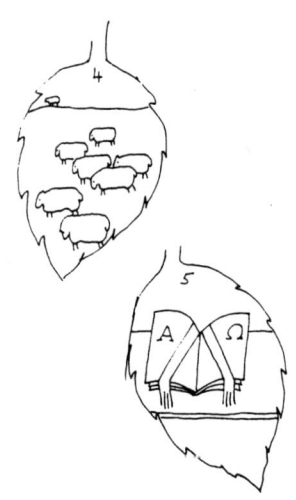

FOURTH SUNDAY OF EASTER
How can you tell your mom or your dad's voice? How do you really know it's them? When do they call you? Jesus talked about the shepherds of his day: They really knew their sheep by name, and the sheep recognized the shepherd's voice. That story was to tell us the same thing—Jesus loves each one of us, by name. He is as close as a mom or dad.

FIFTH SUNDAY OF EASTER
Family members often look alike. "Who is she like? Is he like his dad?" You often hear relatives say this. Who are you like? As followers of the way of Jesus, Christians become alike, too. We try to follow the pattern of his love and care, concern, and forgiveness. Today's gospel tells us: "By the love you have for one another, everyone will know that you are my disciples" (John 13:35).

SIXTH SUNDAY OF EASTER
Letters or cards from friends (especially those overseas) are always welcomed. We open them up quickly to see what they say. We read the words over and over. We share that letter around. Today's gospel is like a letter from Jesus. He has special words for us: I want to give you peace, don't be afraid, I am coming back, my Father loves you, we want to make our home with you.

ASCENSION
When we go away to stay with a friend overnight, our parents always give us some last-minute reminders: "Be good; give me a phone call if you need to be picked up," etc. Jesus had some important final things to say to his friends: "You've been with me for three years now; you've seen what happened; you've heard the Good News. Now you have to be witness to all this." How were his friends as they returned to the city?

SEVENTH SUNDAY OF EASTER
One of the great things about watching a football match, or rooting for any team, is that feeling of being one with so many supporters. Someone scores and everyone stands up and roars and cheers! In a time of sadness, that's how it is too: people come to support each other. Can you think of a time when you felt one with a group? That was a big hope that Jesus had for us; he prayed to his Father for all of us: "Father, may they be one."

PENTECOST
Who is a favorite visitor to your house? Why do you enjoy their coming? What does it do to your home? The friends of Jesus were gathered at someone's place. They were a bit lost, downcast. Then the person who meant most in their lives, Jesus, was present among them. They became alive and enthusiastic and joyful. Other people noticed the change. The spirit of Jesus made all the difference!

49

Paraliturgy to Welcome Ordinary Time
Changing the Color

Preparation
Feature the following toward the front of the room: Paschal candle (lit and decorated with flowers); Easter banner; a table with a white/yellow cloth; Bible, opened on the table.

Welcome
We have just celebrated the fifty days of Easter, a time for remembering that Jesus is alive. We are Easter people, and Alleluia is our song!

It is time now to make changes in our journey. Our church community invites us to enter into "ordinary time" when we ask ourselves:

- What does it mean to be a Christian?
- Is it hard to be a Christian sometimes?
- What does a Christian do?

Today is the day when we change colors from the yellows and golds and reds of Paschal time to the green of ordinary time.

Hymn
"Color the World" (Carey Landry)
(While this is being sung, children carrying banners of red, gold, yellow, and white process in and form a semi-circle around the table.)

Opening Prayer
Let us pray:
Loving God,
you are the great Artist of our universe.
We praise you for the gift of color in our world.
We thank you for the gift of sight to enjoy color.
We ask that we might bring color and love to the lives of the people around us.
We ask this through Christ our Lord.

Homily
Using an overhead projector, talk about
• the cycle of nature and color changes
• the church's cycle and change of colors.
• changing colors point to something
• we can look for those changes about us
• we can change within.

Reading
Selections from Ecclesiasticus 42:15 to 43:28

Rite
(This ritual involves groups of four children. Take plenty of time with this.)
Play quiet music. Let the actions "speak for themselves."

Group 1
Processes to the front, extinguishing the Paschal candle, removes the flowers and moves the candle to the side.
Group 2
Processes to the front, removes the Easter cloth, folds it up, then covers the table with a green cloth.
Group 3
Processes up to the front, removes the Easter banner and puts up a green banner with a message such as "March on...in the journey of life."
Group 4
Processes to the front with green candles (lit) and an arrangement of green vines and leaves or a variety of interesting green potted plants. Arrange these on the table.
Group 5
Processes up the front with an array of green flags (lots of different shades!). The group with the Easter flags lowers their flags and rolls them up. They move away from the front of the room.

Response
All the children say together, "What is Green?" (from *Hailstones and Halibut Bones*) or invite representatives from a class to reflect on what "green" brings to them in their lives.

Closing Prayer
Let us pray:
Loving God,
you gave us color to mark the times and seasons.
Help us to recognize these new signs in our church community
and to listen to your Word in our everyday life.
We ask this through Christ our Lord.

Mission
Children of _____ School,
leave the yellow and gold and red of Paschal time.
See in the green of ordinary time
a sign of hope
and the way to growth.
Go now, in peace to love and serve the Lord.

Recessional
   Bright music for all to depart, following the green flags (e.g., a selection from the "Four Seasons" by Vivaldi or some stirring trumpet music).

Follow-up Activities
   1. Read all the color poems from *Hailstones and Halibut Bones*.
   2. Visit a paint shop/collect color charts: how many shades of green are there?
   3. Have a green day: wear green clothes, eat green food, arrange a "green-thumbs" (gardening) activity.
   4. Conduct a survey to find the most popular shade of green.
   5. Visit a florist or nursery. Look at the variety of green plants.
   6. Make a collection of "Green Favorite Things."
   7. Which countries use green in their national flags?
   8. Why should we plant more green trees to help our environment?
   9. Have a look at a set of green vestments in your church.
   10. Take a green potted plant to a nearby nursing home.

Easter Activities Checklist

1. Take a walk to your parish church and look at the photos of the neophytes: the new Christians, the Easter banners, the Easter symbols of font, candle, and the church adornments.

2. Make contact with the neophytes: display their photos, invite them to speak to your group.

3. Since Easter is the time of festival for the church, it is the most appropriate time for sacramental preparation. Ideally, first communion and confirmation should be scheduled sometime during the fifty days. Your school might also wish to organize an Easter anointing of the sick. It is time, too, for blessings: the use of Easter water is a strong tradition in our church.

4. Display an Easter candle in a prominent place in your school. Encourage the classes to be involved in the adornment of it throughout the fifty days (seven weeks). Light the candle each day, if possible. Have a prayer service around it.

5. Do a theme on baptism: refer to infant baptism, the *Rite of Christian Initiation of Adults*, and the *Christian Initiation of Children Who Have Reached Catechetical Age*.

6. Invite one of the R.C.I.A. team members to talk about the document with your staff and discuss the implications of this for your religious education program, especially R.C.I.C.

7. Talk about the Lectionary and explain, simply, its layout. Then show the class the Lectionary for Masses with children.

8. Enthrone the class Bible in a place of reverence. Encourage the children to care for this place. Display an Easter candle.

9. Do a unit of work on the early Christian community and its lifestyle (Acts of the Apostles).

10. Do a unit of work on the sacraments of initiation (baptism, confirmation, eucharist). Talk about the work of special ministers; make cards for the ministers to the sick to hand out to the sick/elderly.

11. Mount a display of baptismal/first communion certificates.

Your Parish—
An Easter Parish

An Easter People

The liturgies of the Easter eucharists remind us that we are to praise God "with greater joy than ever in this Easter season." Because in Christ

"a new age has dawned,
the long reign of sin is ended,
a broken world has been renewed,
people are, once again, made whole."
(*Preface of Easter, IV*)

But, we may well ask, is this reflected in our own lives and to the world around us? For us twentieth century believers, the challenge is, as never before, to be an Easter people.

So, when are we Easter people?

1. When the Paschal event touches our lives. "All I want is to know Christ and to experience the power of his resurrection" (Philippians 3:9).
2. When the spirit of joy and hope can pervade the "ups and downs" of life.

3. When we live with a new vision, glimpsing life beyond death, thirsting for the "new heaven and new earth" (Revelation 21:1ff).

4. When we realize that we are a pilgrim church, a people of journey, of change and uncertainty.

5. When we accept the human face of the church and our responsibility in shaping its future.

6. When we look back upon our exodus/passover experiences and live as a people of the new covenant.

7. When we have learned to enter into celebration, realizing our gift as a priestly people.

8. When our lives bear witness to the Good News that we are a liberated people.

9. When we dare to be different: to witness that Jesus transforms lives.

Why an Easter People?
As a Christian community, we have lived in the shadow of cross and crucifixion, passion and death. Have we really moved beyond this to new life and resurrection? It is a puzzle as to why Easter "stops" on Easter Sunday. So, we may well reflect, why should a parish be an Easter people?

1. Because each Sunday is the day of resurrection (it ought not be seen in terms of obligation). For the early church it was that weekly celebration of the Lord's Day that gave the Christian community its identity, its vitality, and hope in the presence of the risen savior.

2. Because the sacraments are encounters with Christ, the risen Lord, who touches the lives of his people at these graced moments on the journey.

3. Because an Easter people is a community of concerned Christians. Paul talks about being "body of Christ" and that's what we strive for—to bring Christ to one another (1 Corinthians 12:27ff).

4. Because new Christians (neophytes) need a "sponsoring" community of Easter people with whom they can share stories, break bread, and be drawn into ministry.

5. Because, through conversion, we have accepted Christ and become a "chosen race, a royal priesthood, a people set apart" (1 Peter 1:9ff).

6. Because, in the kingdom, Christ's values are our values. Thirsting for this kingdom means a total commitment to him.

7. Because, realizing and rejoicing in our own gifts, we have placed these at the service of the community.

8. Conscious of being "one in Christ," we work toward unity within the Christian church.

The Catechumenate
The catechumenate proposes a blueprint for transforming a community into an Easter people. It offers the opportunity of ongoing renewal and communi-

ty formation: mission. This becomes very evident in the final period of the catechumenate, the period of mystagogy, and is highlighted in the following specific areas.

Ministry

R.C.I.A works out of a community model of the church. It insists that the formation of inquirers takes place within the community, drawing upon the varying gifts of its members. This requires training and some gentle encouragement. The witness of Christians serving one another challenges the neophytes to discern and exercise their newfound gifts. The neophytes challenge us in surprising ways: We discover new capabilities, inactive members are challenged, and we grow in the understanding of what it means to "be church," to be missionaries.

Community as "Sponsor"

At initiation, the neophytes move from the smaller catechumenal community into the wider community of parish. They encounter a diversity of people striving to live out their Christian commitment. Now all community members become companions on the journey, sharing faith, offering encouragement, living out the gospel that the neophytes have so recently accepted.

Scripture/Liturgy

Two essential resources of parish renewal are Scripture and liturgy. During the enquiry, catechumenate, and election periods, the parish sees the gradual build up in the use of Scripture and liturgy in the formation of new Christians. (They are dismissed after the homily each Sunday, meeting to reflect further on the Word of God; they celebrate various "rites of passage" within the Sunday liturgy.) After Easter, the post-baptismal catechesis takes place within the Sunday eucharist, based on the Scriptures of Paschal time, and is directed towards the whole community—neophytes and congregation alike. Thus, the parish is challenged:

- to offer perceptive and well-planned liturgies;
- to celebrate with energy and exuberance;
- to be a community that openly welcomes its new members.

Since it is in community that we meet the risen Lord, then let the Easter liturgies be festive almost to the point of "exhausting" the parish!

Making Your Parish Church an Easter Church

Liturgical Visuals

Banners and other visuals are considered essential components in liturgy. They help to set a joyful atmosphere of prayer, welcome, and community caring. They aid reflection and understanding of the scripture of the day. The ministry of their creation involves the community. They remain after the celebration as a reminder of what has been said, and what needs to be done.

Visuals may be altar or lectern hangings, banners, overheads, slides, or 3-D displays (which may include symbolic flora in place of the usual flower arrangements). Dance and drama may be part of a liturgy, and if this is so, then the settings and costumes for these also need to be considered.

However, not all of these visuals would be used at once, as too many symbols used simultaneously cancel each other out. A carefully integrated liturgy would contain some of the elements in proportion to the main event—the eucharist—to enhance rather than to overshadow it.

The preparation of the visual environment for meaningful liturgy is in itself a process of education and learning.

Art in Worship

In liturgy we are dealing with things both "seen" and "unseen." Music and song have been the only consistent arts incorporated in liturgy down through the centuries. The visual arts were more or less essential elements (not decoration) until around the 18th century. Gradually sanctuaries and vestments became more cluttered with meaningless decoration.

After the Second Vatican Council, much of this decoration was swept away and the environment became almost sterile, cleared of everything but basic liturgical symbols. Since Vatican II, people have gradually come to realize that what is "seen" is an important lead to what is "unseen." Thus a new search for powerful visual symbols has begun. We live in a "visual" age; today we recognize the need for local contemporary symbols.

All the arts are important and necessary elements of liturgy. "You must love the Lord your God with all your heart, with all your soul, with all your mind, and with all your strength (Mark 12:29-30). The act of artistic creation (an important liturgical ministry) is a search for truth and a form of prayer in its own right. Religious artists—musicians, singers, dancers, actors, poets, painters, sculptors, or designers—strive to interpret, understand, and internalize the Word of God in order to create a work of art with contextual, audio, and visual symbols. The arts, intrinsic elements in liturgy, add a rich dimension at once soul-stirring and joyful, even magnificent. Paschal time, the climax of the church year, invites the richest of liturgical celebrations.

Sign and Symbol

At this time in history we are looking again at the ancient meanings of symbols. They can be found all around us in our daily lives. How do we define "sign" and "symbol"?

A sign has only one meaning; it points to one thing—"stop," "exit," etc.

A symbol has many layers of meaning, experienced in one reality but moving us to a deeper reality whom we call God. A living symbol is never static, but must evolve over a period of time or it reverts to a "sign." The symbol must be grounded in current social, cultural, and political contexts. What is symbolic for one culture may have little meaning in another.

New meanings for symbols emerge from within people's lived experience. The Christian looks at this *lived* reality in the light of the gospels. Symbols are about life. The cyclic Easter event and Paschal time is the great life event of the church year.

In earlier agrarian societies, certain local natural symbols of people, places, and objects, as seen and experienced in daily life, served as a reminder of the world "beyond" and were used in religious rituals. Some of these symbolic shapes held and still hold common meanings to all peoples. For instance, the circle always indicates some form of spiritual, eternal being. The Christian cross consists of a vertical line, which symbolizes transcendence, and a horizontal line symbolizing earthly things.

In the Easter experience, the resurrection might be symbolized by a "living cross," the tree of life.

Contemporary Symbols

Certain natural symbols of the ancient agrarian societies used in biblical texts still have meaning in our contemporary technological context although those old meanings have changed. We come to identify their contemporary meaning by careful observation, by a keen awareness of things around us, and by reflecting on their meaning in our own lives and the lives of others. But natural symbols describing our human condition tell only part of the story.

In what way can we use people as symbol in the Easter experience? Eggs, butterflies, Easter bunnies, spring flowers alone do little to explain the meaning of the resurrection in the lives of people. The gospels abound in images of "new life" as seen in the experiences of people through their contact with Jesus: the women at the tomb, those on the road to Emmaus, and so on. Newspapers, TV, cartoons, and magazine articles might help to identify the local experience of these Easter symbols, along with group discussion, study, and reflection.

A few possible natural symbols with contemporary Easter time and catechumenate application are:

Fire: Both urban and country areas experience fire: its power, warmth, necessity, or destructive power.

Water: What is our experience of water in times of drought, flood, need, thirst? And in holiday time?

Wind: We experience those strong spring winds (Easter time falls in the springtime).

Bread: It is still a staple diet in Western countries. But what does it mean to those whose staple diet is rice or sweet potato?

Wine: Still a secular symbol of conviviality and celebration. But it, too, has its destructive side.

Oil: Necessary for cooking and as a base of many products, including those that protect us from the strong summer rays; fuel for warmth.

The Frontispiece

In the banner which is this book's frontispiece, Jesus and his "ministers" are clothed in white. The neophytes are as beautiful new flowers turning toward the light—Jesus—as they grow along the fertile roadside. This road symbolizes the life journey we all travel (our "road to Emmaus"). At Pentecost the figure of Jesus becomes a white silhouette on which the flame of the Spirit is placed.

The next section links parts of the Easter banner with the Sunday gospel readings. (See chart on pages 62-63.)

An Easter People Commissioned
At the first Pentecost, the followers of Jesus were "surprised" by the gift of the Spirit. Impelled by the Good News that Jesus is risen, they put their gifts and talents at the service of the community. They were the first Easter people.

This same Spirit is at work among us. During the fifty days of Easter, we are invited to reflect on our gifts and talents. At Pentecost we commit ourselves to some form of ministry. Paul reminds us, of course, that not all are called to "front line" works in the parish. There is a variety of gifts and *all* are important (1 Corinthians 12:4).

Pentecost Sunday is an appropriate occasion to commission the whole parish. Each community member is encouraged to commit his or her giftedness to some particular task in the parish for the coming year. Further details are given in the chapter on the catechumenate, Chapter 3.

Celebrating Easter as a Family
The child's first and lasting impressions of Easter take place within the family circle. They sense "something different" taking place as Easter approaches and the mythical Easter bunny catches the imagination. There seems to be a lot of church-going and, even there, the rituals seem somehow different—certainly longer! The Holy Week-Easter ceremonies are undeniably adult experiences. So, where does that leave families?

Much can be done within the home to celebrate the fifty days of Easter. Bright decorations with lots of "alleluias" can adorn the family living areas. The centerpiece might be the family's own Easter candle, which is lit during meal times. Other symbols such as rabbits, Easter cards, painted eggs, fancy hats, and growing seeds might be included in the display. This becomes a talking point, then, with friends and visitors.

Families are encouraged to support these parish/school activities:

- participating in children's Liturgy of the Word sessions and following through these discussions back at home;
- talking about the banners and Easter symbols with the child. This helps to make the child observant;
- taking an interest in the school's Easter activities. Feature the Easter posters/pictures that do come home in the school bag;
- listening to Easter stories at home;
- remembering the family celebrations of the sacraments of initiation (baptism, confirmation, eucharist). Display photos, certificates, dates, and any other memorabilia;
- recognize the presence of neophytes in your parish:
  —send a card of welcome/congratulations
  —introduce your family after Mass
  —invite them for tea or coffee in your home and ask a few other parishioners to come along
  —mention the neophytes by name, when your family prays

	TEXT	SYMBOLS	REFLECTION
Easter Sunday	...they killed him by hanging him on a tree, yet three days afterwards God raised him to life and allowed him to be seen...we have eaten and drunk with him after his resurrection from the dead—and he has ordered us to proclaim this to his people...(First reading, Acts 10:34, 37-38).	Jesus stands bathed in light in a field of "flowers," the neophytes. (Highlight each weekly symbol with a spotlight so that the visual is easier to understand.)	He is risen!
Second Sunday of Easter	The disciples were filled with joy when they saw the Lord, and he said to them again, "Peace be with you" (John 20:19-31).	The new Christians turn their faces toward the risen Lord as flowers turn toward the light.	We experience growth in our own personal relationship with the Lord, and individually we respond to him.
Third Sunday of Easter	Then they told their story of what happened on the road and how they had recognized him at the breaking of the bread (Luke 24:13-35).	A picnic in the country, or by the roadside, where we share our bread in peace and happiness. (The breaking of bread in a contemporary context.)	All three gospels for Cycles A, B, and C are about sharing meals: road to Emmaus, his coming among them, breakfast by the water. In all stories, Jesus was recognized when he broke bread. We recognize him in community at the "breaking of bread" in Eucharist.
Fourth Suday of Easter	I am the gate...I have come so they may have life and have it to the full (John 10:1-10).	The gate, through which I must pass, and the path along which I must go.	This path and this gate are our way to our own "resurrection."

Fifth Sunday of Easter	I am the vine and you are the branches, says the Lord; he who lives in me, and I in him will bear much fruit, alleluia (Communion Antiphon, John 15:5). Note: This text has been chosen because it "sums up" the relationship between the risen Lord and the community, and is thus appropriate for the three cycles.	The grapevine as seen in our contemporary vineyards along the roadside.	We contemplate three meanings of the vine: a) the grafting or interlocking into the life of God—the relationship between Jesus and the Father; b) between Jesus and us; c) community bonding—one with each other. living out the Easter faith.
Sixth Sunday of Easter	Anybody who receives my commandments and keeps them will be one who loves me; and anybody who loves me will be loved by my Father and I shall love him and show myself to him (John 14:15-21).	The gardener represents those in the catechumenate ministry. The flower he carefully holds symbolizes the new Christian.	As the gardener lovingly ministers to the new flowers, so does the Spirit lovingly care for those who keep the commandment of love.
Ascension	He replied, "It is not for you to know times or dates that the Father has decided by his own authority, but you will receive power when the Holy Spirit comes on you, and then you will be my witnesses...to the ends of the earth" (First reading, Acts 1:1-11).	Hand of God and rays of light mark the path of Jesus' ascent into heaven, and the descent of his Spirit on us.	We have the experience of saying goodbye, and we learn to accept what is to come.
Seventh Sunday of Easter	I believe that I shall see the good things of the Lord in the land of the living (Responsorial Psalm 26).	The clouds and the hand of God symbolize the heavens.	We look forward to the coming of the Spirit. We are earthbound but we have the promise of things to come.
Pentecost Suday	Lord, send out your Spirit and renew the face of the earth (Responsorial Psalm 103).	The "flame of the Spirit" appear around the figure of Jesus or over the heart of Jesus.	The Spirit of Jesus enflames and enlightens the whole earth.

- read the Sunday Scriptures together as a family. Decide upon some practical action as a result;
- give the Bible a place of reverence in your home. Display Easter symbols for fifty days;
- organize a get-together of your children's godparents and sponsors.
- take an interest in your parish R.C.I.C.

Finally, families might find ways to take Easter to others. Just as the early Christian community was caught up in the mystery and excitement of Jesus, risen among them, we too can bring joy to elderly relatives, sick neighbors, friends we have not seen for ages, or just making time for a weekend away with the family. How can we be Good News for others? As Pentecost approaches, thought might be given to the particular mission of each family. It is an opportunity to take seriously the parish initiative to make Pentecost a true "missioning Sunday" for everyone.

Parish Checklist

1. Publish excerpts about your parish community and its life, and various groups in your weekly bulletin between Easter and Pentecost.

2. Display photos of the new Christians and their families or sponsors in the foyer of your church.

3. Leave a box beneath the photos for parishioners to write notes or cards of welcome to the neophytes.

4. Invite everyone to wear name tags during the fifty days to enable people to make new contacts in the parish. Decorate the new Christians' name tags in a recognizable way.

5. Establish groups to welcome people at your church doors during this time. Greet people, hand them a bulletin, talk with them.

6. Hold a seminar for your parish liturgy team. Review the year and make plans for the future.

7. Revise your liturgical rosters: readers, special ministers, collectors, presentation of the gifts, etc. Look to the needs of the community in this area.

8. Invite families to contribute flowers or donations to make your church festive for the fifty days.

9. Arrange a renewal of faith course during Easter time. Reflect on the meaning of the sacraments of initiation as one of the sessions.

10. Make a special feature of all of the baptisms during this season.

11. Publicize the parish policy on the sacraments of initiation.

12. Work at improving the proclamations of the Word at your liturgical gatherings.

13. Invite the readers to be part of the entrance procession at Sunday and weekday Eucharists.

14. Form Easter reflection/discussion groups.

15. Look at the possibility of having a children's Liturgy of the Word during this Easter period (see page 27).

6

Litugical Visuals

The Liturgy Group
The Pastor, D.R.E., Director of Music Ministries (or organist, choir director, etc.) banner/visual maker, flower person, dance and drama coordinator, Renew and catechumenate coordinators ideally form a liturgy group. They could invite others who are interested to join them, and encourage them to provide ideas and contributions in various ways.

Design Procedure
When designing Easter banners, audiovisuals, or 3-D displays, it is desirable to be aware of a number of things. First of all, be very familiar with *Environment and Art in Catholic Worship*, a document issued in 1978 by the Bishops Committee on the Liturgy of the United States Catholic Conference. It gives clear, practical principles that can guide you in creating and using visual art in liturgy. Once you know the guidelines, here is one suggested procedure:

1. Read through the lectionary texts with a group of interested people. Ask the group to reflect on each Sunday reading in the light of their own experiences. Begin this practice well beforehand; planning and making visuals takes time. Find a common theme developed in the Scripture readings over the Lent/Easter season.

2. Having found a focus, try to identify contemporary symbols that might be appropriate. Be aware of the time of the year in which Easter falls. In the northern hemisphere, it falls in spring/summer, but in the southern hemisphere, it is usually late autumn/early winter. Observe the natural signs and colors around at the time. Flowering or fruiting local plants could help in the selection of shapes and colors. Seasonal activities such as secular festivals, sports, and agricultural pursuits may be worth noting and used in some way. The local environment has much to offer by way of symbol.

3. Decide which of the arts you feel should be included, and in what proportion. This will depend on the skills available, what "materials" are in season, and the enthusiasm of the community. For example, a profusion of certain local flowers may establish the main focus for a celebration.

4. With the choir leader, select music and songs appropriate to the seasonal theme.

5. If banners are to be the focus, assign specific tasks to each sewer, and oversee the making of the banner.

6. Organize the hanging of the banner before the liturgy. Remove it at the agreed-upon time and store it carefully.

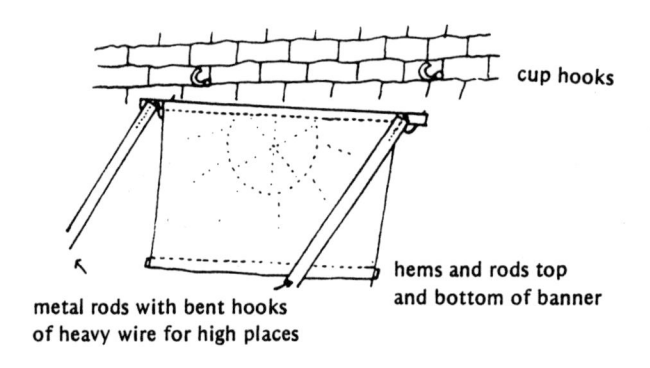

Banners

1. The number and size of banners depends on the space available. Mounts can easily be fitted in such a way that they are unnoticeable when not in use.

2. Existing lighting should be noted, as it can affect colors on banners and displays. The colors of the walls, carpets, and other fittings, and the architectural style also need to be considered.

3. Banners need not be costly to be beautiful. Good quality, reasonably priced no-iron fabrics, with symbols stitched (not glued) to the backing banner will ensure sturdy banners that will take constant handling and folding with ease.

4. One cost-cutting exercise is to make backing banners in white (or red) gabardine or similar material. Symbols may be pinned on these and removed easily. Such backings can be used for most liturgical seasons and feast days. The symbols may be made of felt if a small size, or poplin fabric mounted on vilene (for strength) if they are large. The pins will not be noticeable.

5. Let people know donated fabrics, braids, lace, etc. would be appreciated. People are very generous if they feel their donations will be put to good use.

6. Banners with symbols that build up over a period are invaluable. Such a banner program creates a sense of anticipation and climax. The symbol of the day is seen in context with what has gone before.

7. It is advisable to remove any visuals at a suitable time after their season. Eye rest is just as important as the visual. If left up too long, people cease to see visuals, and they lose their impact.

What to avoid:
- Use of children's artwork for adult liturgies. It does not necessarily challenge adults, but for children's liturgies it is invaluable.
- Words on banners. A thoughtful and well-designed visual has no need of words. Words focus on one meaning and impede the discovery of further levels of meaning. If an explanation is necessary the first time around, then place it in the parish bulletin.

Method for Transferring Design and Making Banners

1. Make a complete color plan of the design on paper. Use the designs in this book or trace all parts of suitable photos, magazine illustrations, cartoons, etc. *But remember, no lettering!*

2. Transfer (trace or photocopy) the design onto an overhead transparency.

3. Enlarge the design to the size required by moving the overhead projector away from the wall on which you have attached a large sheet of paper (for the pattern) and hung your backing banner (to record the position of pattern pieces).

4. Trace the design twice, using chalk that will rub off the backing later. Number each design so that you know which pattern piece goes where.

5. Now you are able to estimate how much of each fabric color you will need. Purchase fabric and cut out the design pieces. Prepare the backing banner to the desired size. Join wide banner pieces down the middle and press the seam open. Do not hem the sides or top or bottom edges yet.

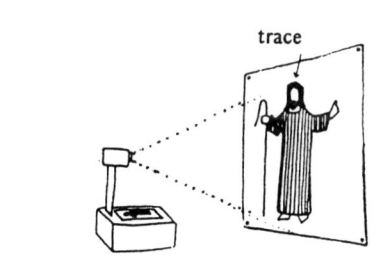

6. Pin the design pieces in their correct order on the backing. Pin the backing around a rod at the top temporarily and hang the banner in its final position to check that all is well with the design. This is the time to move anything that is incorrectly placed, or change any color that does not "carry" when seen from a distance.

7. If the banner is a large one, design pieces can be more easily held in place for sewing if spray-glued lightly on the back before placing them on the backing. But test first on a sample of fabric; the glue marks may show through thin or semi-transparent fabrics.

8. Iron the fabric pieces carefully before zig-zag stitching over the raw edges. This ensures that the fabric pieces are completely flat on the backing, and will not sag when hung vertically.

9. Carefully iron the finished banner, then fold over each side edge and straight-stitch them.

10. Fold over the top and bottom edges of the banner, allowing enough room to insert rods. Stitch.

Note: If banners have a figure added, make this separately. Cut out the fabric pieces and attach each in order onto a backing of vilene. It is easier to sew around all the small pieces involved when working this way. If you wish to pad a figure to make it appear three-dimensional, slit the vilene on the back of the area to be padded and insert thin batting (the type used for quilts). With needle and thread, pull together the edges of the slits so the batting will not fall out. Then, when the figure is complete, it may be attached to the backing banner by hand, or machine, or if preferred it may just be pinned in place.

Rods: Get good quality, strong metal rods; cheap plastic-coated metal rods sag under much weight. Thin wooden rods also sag. Thick wooden rods may be suitable but their appearance would be enhanced with decorative ends. Otherwise trim the rods to fit the banner. (Pages 70-72 provide illustrations.)

The Vertical Banner

Stage 1

Stage 2

Stage 3

Build up of fabric design units. The design may be broken into smaller areas of colour if desired

Figure of Jesus for vertical banner

1 skin colour

2 hair and beard

3 stitch or penline features

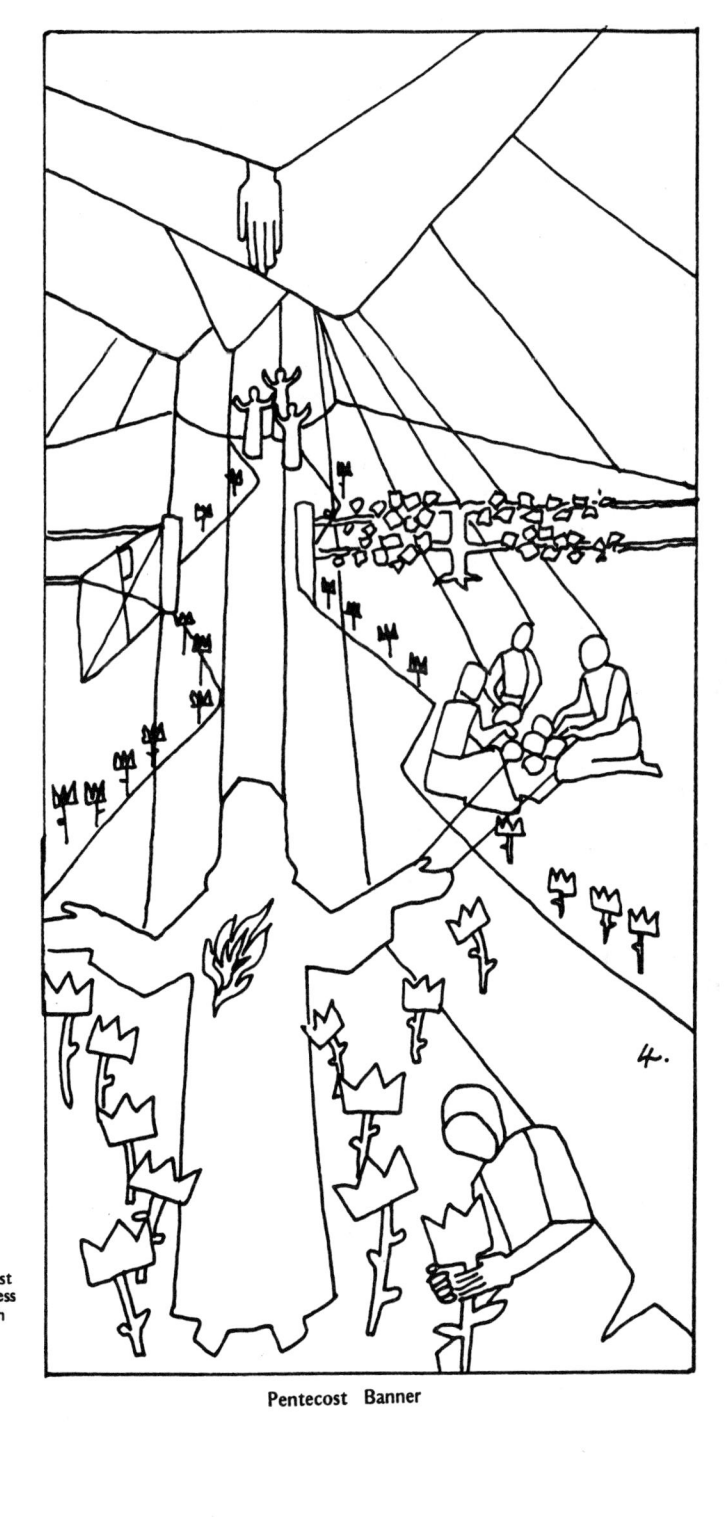

4 robe, hands feet wounds

5 Pentecost featureless but with flame added

Pentecost Banner

71

The Horizontal Banner

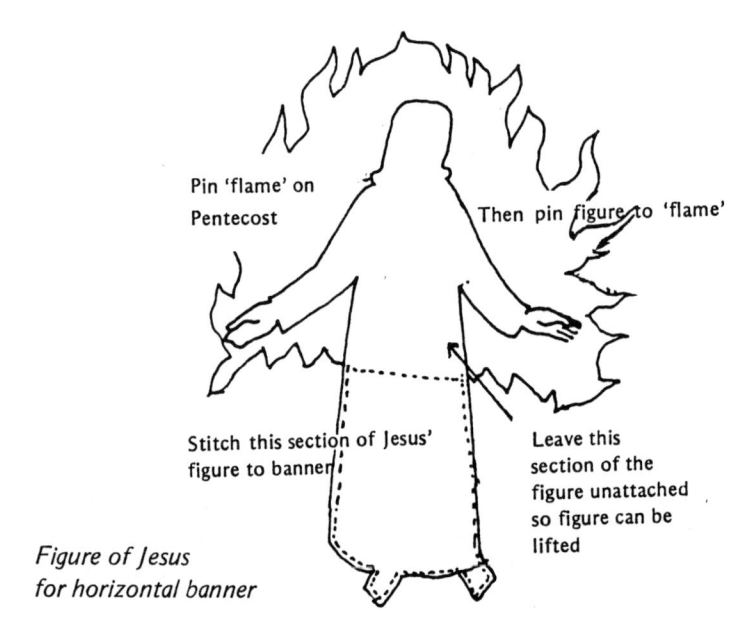

Pin 'flame' on Pentecost

Then pin figure to 'flame'

Stitch this section of Jesus' figure to banner

Leave this section of the figure unattached so figure can be lifted

Figure of Jesus for horizontal banner

Audiovisuals
The screen for audiovisuals and slides ideally should be in such a place that it can be covered or removed when not in use. Prominent unused screens look ugly and can be distracting during liturgy. The position of the projector is also important. People moving around a projector, and the light that issues from it, can be very distracting. One way to prevent this is to place low screens around the work area on three sides to the height of a seated projectionist.

Some fortunate churches have built-in provisions for audiovisual equipment, and consideration should be given to this when planning a new church.

Good overheads can be hard to find. It is good to prepare your own. A photocopier that copies onto transparencies is a real asset. Transparencies can be hand colored for greater impact. It is possible to overlay all or part of transparencies to make up a composite picture. However, no more than three layers can be used for clarity. Cut away sections where further layers are needed.

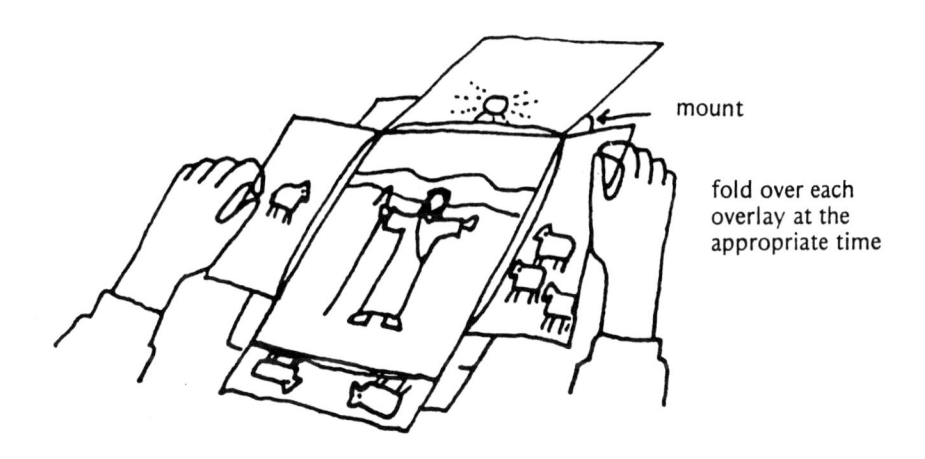

mount

fold over each overlay at the appropriate time

Find out if you have a calligrapher in the parish. Ask him or her to print out hymns, etc., in black or colored inks of good quality on the transparencies, and you will have a work of art worthy of the house of God. Avoid using rough and ready transparencies for this reason. Think ahead. Plan ahead.

Great care should be taken with the content of slides and overheads. Often commercially produced material is out of place for local use. How much more meaning a reflective post-communion slide has when the viewer can personally identify with it!

Note: It is a good idea to record in photographs and by other means all visuals used during a liturgical season. The growth of involvement in liturgy is very encouraging not only to members of a parish community but to other parishes who are beginning an arts-integrated liturgy of their own.

3-D Displays

3-D displays can sometimes be used alone or alongside banners or audiovisuals, as long as they follow through the liturgical themes. Pots with native or local flowering or fruiting plants or trees may be used in association with other visuals.

3-D displays may be arranged either in front of or at the side of the altar, or at the entrance of the church, but should never hinder movement, obscure vision, or give the impression of clutter. All visuals must be removed at the conclusion of the celebration for which they were intended.

Easter 3-D Display Suggestions:
1. Select something that can "grow" over the Easter season, e.g., a branch that has "leaves" added each week. There could be special prayers for community members or for the new Christians written on colored cards cut into leaf shapes. This branch could be "planted" inside the main doors where the community has access to it.
2. Sow some fast growing seeds in plant boxes and plant them out into pots at Easter. Have someone tend them and let the community watch them grow. Refer to them in the homily, etc.
3. Plant a new shrub or tree each time a new catechumenate group reaches Initiation. These could be planted in church or school grounds, but ideally they should be where the community can see them growing.
4. Use special local tree or flower arrangements as much as possible. Which flowers symbolize Pentecost in your region?

Ascension
Bring in a large rock and put it in a central place on Ascension eve. Before Ascension Mass, drape over the rock a man's coat (or if you want to be more traditional use a draped cloth like a biblical robe). Also include a pair of men's sandals, and perhaps a knapsack. Then let the people make of those symbols what they will.

Pentecost
Instead of a banner you may like to:
1. Have Pentecost flags carried in the entrance or final procession. Have the carriers of these thread them on cord and drape them along the front fence of the church. Or make a large flag, and place on it flames of the Spirit. Mount the flag on a flag pole in the church grounds on Pentecost morning.
2. Have a special "dismissal rite."
3. Make paper "Pentecost flames" and thread them on a fishing line. Attach several lines over the front doors so they flutter in the breeze above the heads of the community as they enter and leave the church.
4. Bake special Pentecost cakes (or other foods) and share these after Mass in the community gathering. Include traditional Pentecost foods of other cultures if you can.
5. Play a tape of the sound of the wind blowing during the first reading (Acts).

Dance and Drama
At present, many dioceses do not include these arts to any extent in the liturgy. But if they do, it needs to be well planned, rehearsed, and costumed appropriately so they can be integrated into the liturgy and do not become just a "show." Their message can be very powerful if they are properly planned. There are many skilled people in the community who would love to use this gift to demonstrate their love for God.

7

The Easter Journey—Implications

Plan for 90—Not 40!
In recent years our parish experiences of Lent have deepened. We've recognized the sign posts of these forty days as a time to

- probe the great events of salvation history
- pray and reflect on the great healing stories of
    the woman at the well
    the man born blind
    the raising of Lazarus
- focus on
    supper........................ Holy Thursday
    sacrifice...................... Good Friday
    sacrament................ Holy Saturday

The challenge ahead of us is to take the fifty days of Easter just as seriously. We are sensitized to the dangers of "lenten overkill." Can we turn our attention now to the panorama of the ninety days? This is planning on a grand scale. The church proposes this strategy as the basis for community renewal and mission, yet:

1. Do we *see* the signs of the 50 days of Easter in our communities?
2. Do we recognize the gift of new life through the presence of the neophytes?
3. Does the community accept its responsibility as "sponsor" to these new Christians?
4. Do we perceive a deeper understanding of ministries and *mission* in the community?
5. Do our liturgies reflect the festive nature of Paschal time?
6. Do we make visible the great symbols of initiation, e.g., adorned font, Paschal candle, and holy oils?

A New Look at the "Basic" Sacraments
Since the re-establishment of the catechumenate in what now amounts to hundreds of dioceses throughout the world, a new approach toward the sacraments of initiation has been developing. The most appropriate time for their reception, the theology underlying each of these sacraments, and their pastoral and liturgical implications; all these bear reexamination.

While Vatican II initiated the restoration of all the sacraments, it is the document on R.C.I.A. that has challenged us to review our pastoral practices. The introductions to the revised rites of the sacraments outline their theology and vision; but has this been largely overlooked? For example, the revised rite on infant baptism gives direction; but what practical procedures have we adopted back in our parishes?

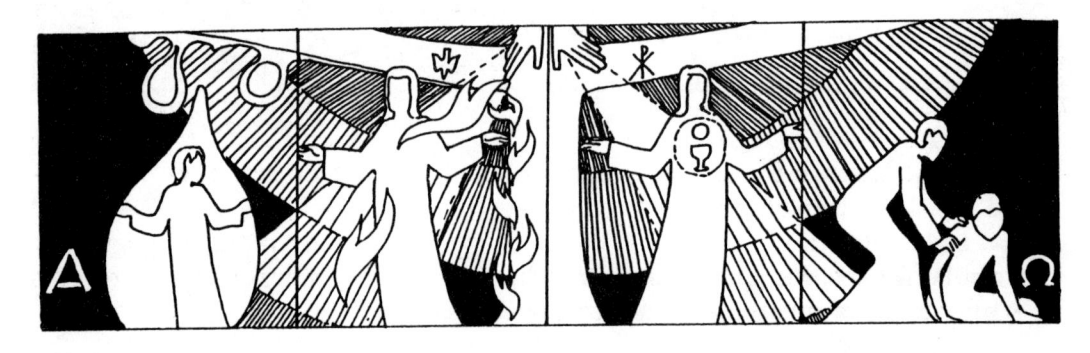

Living the Easter sacraments is not just a theological idea for catechumens who have joined the faith community. It should be the experience of all Christians. Sacraments are celebrations of the whole community. Routine rituals, carried out in private, have little impact on the community. Living the Easter sacraments is to live and deepen the faith commitment of everyone, to be a people of mission.

There is a richness in the sacraments that does not answer to words or explanations. They are awe-inspiring mysteries of commitment and encounter with the risen Lord that cannot be categorized or analysed in computer printouts. What significance do the sacraments have in the lives of Christians?

There are recurring questions: greatly increased numbers receive the eucharist, but has the quality of Christian life improved? The dwindling numbers at reconciliation! Is sin on the decline? Our churches are packed for first communion and confirmation, but what about the following Sunday?

The catechumenate offers a model and a process for effectively celebrating sacraments. These principles can be used especially in the celebration of baptism, confirmation, eucharist, and reconciliation.

1. The sacraments are to be celebrated publicly—no longer are they the preserve of private ceremonies.
2. The community is to be involved, both in the preparation and actual celebration.
3. Lay ministries are to evolve; Vatican II spelled the end of the "clericalization" of the sacraments.
4. Catechesis is to be based on the lectionary; the Scriptures lead us to reflect upon the great mysteries as encounters with the risen Lord.
5. The ecclesial nature of sacrament is to be emphasized. We belong to the "body of Christ," not an exclusive club.

All sacraments are genuine moments of renewal and rededication. It is here that we encounter the risen Lord and his transforming presence. This was experienced time and again in the first communities as they retold Jesus' words and remembered his actions. They experienced what it meant to have "hearts burning within them" as he spoke to them on their journey. It was not magic; it was the life-giving power of God's love flowing into their hearts.

This is a deep mystery; those touched by it were never the same again. Be they a Zacchaeus, or a Paul, or a Mary Magdalene— to encounter the risen Lord either on the road to Emmaus or in the communities of faith, the effect is the same: "It is now no longer I who live, but Jesus Christ lives in me" (Galatians 2:20). This is evident in our catechumenal communities. The same spirit should imbue our rituals of infant baptism, first communion, and confirmation. True, it will take years to shed the many historical accretions. There is no question either of turning the clock back or jettisoning current pastoral practices. Rather, we should be attempting to incorporate the insights of the R.C.I.A. in our pastoral initiatives.

Baptism
The routine, quite anonymous, baptisms of some twenty years ago can have no place in today's community of faith.

The revised rite of infant baptism reflects a different emphasis: It attempts to make of baptism a living Paschal sacrament for all the community. The new rite insists on the preparation of parents and godparents so that they may take part in the rite with understanding. This preparation is the responsibility of the community. "The people of God have an important part to play in the baptism of both children and adults: before and after the celebration of the sacrament, the child has a right to the love and the help of the community" (*Introduction to the Rite of Baptism*, 4).

The child is being baptized into the faith of this community (not the family's private faith). We find our strength in the faith of the church of Jesus Christ.

The task of the parents is even more important. Their role is to form and lead their children to a faith that they freely accept as their own. This is why parents are involved in the preparation of their children for other sacraments of initiation—eucharist and confirmation. The document states: "Christian formation seeks to lead them gradually to learn God's plan in Christ so that they may ultimately accept for themselves the faith in which they have been baptized" (*Introduction to the Rite of Baptism*, 3).

We are asking no more and no less of the parents of a child to be baptized than we ask of the catechumen. The community helps the catechumen to discern the depth of faith, their commitment before they receive the Easter sacraments of initiation. This is precisely what preparation for parents is meant to effect. It is important to understand that the community is not judging their faith but asking them to reflect upon their faith-life and commitment. This process needs sensitivity and certain understanding of those who seem no more than "nominal" Catholics.

Keeping in mind the principles of the catechumenate model, the following checklist may assist parish teams to look at their situation and decide upon certain priorities with regard to infant baptism:

Pastors
1. Visit the families before the celebration.
2. Invite married couples to conduct a baptism program. Provide them with the necessary training.
3. Establish a parish policy about the timing of baptism (e.g., once a month, etc.).
4. Celebrate baptism within the eucharist: a parish Mass, or a special baptism Mass.
5. Use large, bold symbols for the celebration.
6. Arrange a suitable program of preparation with the lay ministers.
7. Give thought to celebrating the sacrament in stages: the ceremony of welcome on one Sunday and the baptism the following Sunday.
8. Introduce the couples to other parishioners.

Lay Ministers
1. Read some current literature on the sacrament of baptism.
2. Conduct the preparation sessions.
3. Arrange for sponsoring couples from the parish as well as the chosen godparents.
4. Announce the forthcoming baptisms in the parish bulletin or on a noticeboard.

5. Reflect, together with the pastor, on the Scripture texts suggested in the rite of baptism.

6. Encourage other parishioners to extend hospitality to the couples involved in the baptism program.

Community
1. Actively welcome the baptismal families.
2. Take an ongoing interest in the families if they live nearby.
3. Become informed about your parish's baptismal policy.
4. Participate as a parish sponsoring couple and encourage others to do the same.

Parents
1. Choose committed Christian godparents.
2. Become acquainted with your local parish community.
3. Become familiar with the parish baptismal policy.
4. Give yourself time.
5. Make contact, later, with the other couples in the baptismal program. Organize a simple get-together.
6. Celebrate the anniversaries of baptism along with birthdays.
7. Display the symbols and photos of this special day.
8. Maintain contact with godparents and the sponsoring couple.
9. Talk over the meaning and implications with your partner.

Confirmation
Confirmation is a sacrament of initiation. This certainly influences the type of catechesis and the pastoral consequences of each parish. The relationship of confirmation to baptism and eucharist needs emphasizing. The theology of baptism provides the principles for understanding those other "moments" of Christian initiation—confirmation and eucharist. The Constitution on the Liturgy called for the revision of the rite of confirmation so that "the ultimate connection which this sacrament has with the whole of Christian initiation should be more lucidly set forth" (paragraph 71). The ensuing revision of August 1971 tried to do this. But the document must be studied in conjunction with the rite of baptism for children (May 1969). Why was the revision necessary?

The decline of the adult catechumenate and its eventual demise in the West left, in its wake, pastoral problems that were never fully faced. The rite of baptism for children was really an adult ritual shortened in a single ceremony. The unity of the sacraments of baptism, confirmation, and eucharist was lost. Separate "theologies" were developed for these sacraments. Their relationship to Easter and the saving love of the risen Lord lost its impact.

Christian initiation involves incorporation into a supportive and believing community that publicly proclaims the gospel of the risen Lord. For confirmation, the community is no less important than for the other sacraments of initiation. It is a celebration of the whole community for the Spirit has been given to all at baptism. In the past there was the suggestion that confirmation somehow "rounded off" baptism—as if baptism was, in itself, incomplete. In the light of the revised rite, it is now clear that baptism and confirmation are closely connected. Confirmation celebrates the fullness of the Spirit given at baptism.

Once again, we have much to learn from looking to the catechumenal model for our parish celebrations of confirmation. Parish teams are invited to consider the following suggestions as they assess needs and establish procedures:

Pastor
1. Establish a policy about the celebration of confirmation in the parish.
2. Ensure that the theology of confirmation is appropriate to the age of the student (e.g., a 12-year-old cannot celebrate this event as commitment).
3. Find ways of involving young people in parish activities.
4. Ensure that confirmation is a celebration of the whole parish.
5. Encourage all parishioners to be actively involved in the program.

Student
1. Give thought as to one's readiness for confirmation.
2. Ask adults what it means to live as a Christian.
3. Develop a close relationship with the sponsor.
4. Accept the responsibilities involved in the program.
5. Ask about your baptism and first communion.

Parents
1. Suggest a sponsor who is able to take an active part in the preparation for confirmation.
2. Spend extra time just talking with your son or daughter.
3. Reflect on the meaning of confirmation in your life.
4. Support the work of the catechists.
5. Recall baptism memories.
6. Act as a group leader.
7. Make this time of preparation a family time.

Sponsor
1. Spend time just talking with the student.
2. Check out the responsibilities of sponsorship.
3. Take time to talk about being Christian and its responsibilities.
4. Take an interest in all the preparatory activities.
5. Update your understanding of confirmation.

Catechist
1. Arrange a comprehensive catechesis of prayer, learning, service, and community experiences.
2. Communicate often with the community via the parish bulletin; explain the variety of activities.
3. Involve many parishioners in a variety of ways.
4. Invite students to make a serious decision about confirmation and its ongoing responsibilities.

Community
1. Volunteer to pray for a student.
2. Take an interest in a neighbor who is to be confirmed.
3. Assist with social functions.
4. Offer to act as a group leader.
5. Reflect on the meaning of confirmation.

Eucharist

We now focus on eucharist in the context of initiation. The washing (in baptism) and the sealing-anointing (of confirmation) are carried out once only in the life of the Christian; but with eucharist it is different.

This was at the heart of the community for the early followers of Jesus. Eucharist was not limited to the idea of "holy communion" as we know it. Eucharist was the full participation in that ritual meal where the risen Lord not only stood among his followers again through assembly and the holy Scriptures, but personally came to them through the consecrated bread and wine. It was the Body and Blood of the Lord himself, something more than the senses could perceive.

It happened each time they assembled; there was no question of obligation here. They came together because they had experienced a freedom unknown and unparalleled in any other circumstance of their lives. All distinctions were set aside. They risked their lives and often paid the supreme penalty to be able to gather around the table of the Lord. Of the great "signs" inherited by the followers of Jesus, this was the summit. They celebrated simply, yet with great dignity. They celebrated it in memory of him and also in memory of their first coming to know him, to be one with him, to com-union with him.

Each time they celebrated, they realized again that Emmaus sign: his presence with them on the journey. How can we capture and sustain that experience for our new Christians? How can we rekindle it for ourselves?

The theology of initiation provides an answer. Eucharist is not an isolated moment in our lives. It is part of the whole process of coming-to-faith and conversion. The simple yet profound phrase of Thomas Aquinas sums up the faith of those who came to know Jesus:

"Not to sight, or touch or taste be credit,
Hearing only do we trust secure."

Eucharist is not a private celebration. Former practices did emphasize eucharist as something personal between "my" God and myself, all others excluded. The community at eucharist was imaged as dozens of separated cells encapsulated in worlds of their own.

Vatican II re-emphasized the essentials of eucharistic celebration, though a trickle of changes over the years had paved the way for these reforms. In an atmosphere of deep reverence, while a group of friends remembered a liberation that formed a people, Jesus took bread, blessed it, broke it, and gave it to them. Thus a pattern of life was set in motion for a new liberation. This was the new covenant, the one that would form yet another people, but this time a priestly people set apart and to be called "God's own" (1 Peter 2:9).

And we become part of this priestly people when we surrender our lives through conversion so that the risen Lord can take them, bless them, break them, and give them as eucharist. We are bread that is blessed and broken when conversion and reconciliation leave hearts open to the Paschal message of redemption.

The fifty days of Easter is prime time for reflection on eucharist. In the presence of the neophytes we rejoice in this incredible gift of our God. Their enthusiasm heightens our awareness; our belief unfolds this mystery for them. If ever there is a suitable time for celebrating first communion, it is the Easter season! It is a time of joy and festivity; its focus is upon initiation; the Easter lectionary provides a wealth of catechetical material. Because it is the time of mystagogia, the unfolding of mysteries, this seems an eminently suitable season for parents to open up the treasures of eucharist for their child.

Following the catechumenal model again, what directions are possible for celebrating eucharist in community?

Pastor
1. Get to know the families who have children preparing for first communion.
2. Initiate the children to the eucharist by holding small group celebrations so that they can see what is happening.
3. Review your parish communion procedures. Perhaps the congregation may need a reminder.
4. Look to ways of distributing communion under both kinds in the parish.

Catechist
1. Inform parishioners of the names of children celebrating first communion.
2. Arrange an appropriate catechesis that enables the child to take his or her place at Sunday eucharist.
3. Involve the family in the preparation of their child.

Parents
1. Sit near the front of the church so that the child can see all that happens at Mass.
2. Pray with the child at home.
3. As a family, talk about what the Mass means to you.
4. Take time for storytelling.
5. Make your family meal a special moment for sharing with each other.
6. Follow through the catechist's suggestions.
7. Arrange a treat after Sunday Mass.

Child
1. Learn how to use a simple Mass book.
2. Come up to the priest at communion time for a special blessing.
3. Ask about your early childhood; look through photos.

Community
1. Take an interest in the children preparing for first communion.
2. Reflect back on the meaning of the eucharist in your life and how the mystery has gradually unfolded.
3. Take an interest in a neighbor who is preparing for first communion; share stories about your special day.

Reconciliation—for an Easter People
A fresh understanding of the sacrament of reconciliation emerges when it is viewed against the background of Christian initiation. The theology of the sacraments of initiation forces us to re-think our approach to reconciliation. It can no longer be regarded as a sacrament of convenience or that once a year obligation. In situations where we fracture ourselves from the community through sin, reconciliation celebrates a "re-membering" with that community and a recommitment to our baptismal promises.

We might well ponder the following:

1. Even though we have a sacrament of reconciliation, we may not take our baptismal promises lightly. We are committed to Christian discipleship—not club membership.
2. The celebration of reconciliation focuses on a loving and merciful God. This calls for a positive approach to our sinfulness.
3. The forgiving/healing stories of Jesus reaffirm
    • his all-forgiving power
    • his reaffirmation of what was good in each person
    • his call to celebrate our return.

4. Reconciliation is related to life both in our eucharistic community and back in our everyday world.

5. Reconciliation is more than a ritual. We make and live the difficult decision to be reconciled.

6. The new rite sets a framework by which one can experience the Lord's mercy.

7. Reconciliation is an ongoing process rather than an event.

8. Reconciliation follows a scriptural model:
    - Jesus unconditionally accepted his failed friends;
    - he opened their hearts—restored their confidence ("Peace be with you");
    - he did not remove the difficulties of being his followers (he showed them his wounds).

Panels for the Sacraments of Initiation and Reconciliation
This set of panels has been designed to assist communities highlight the sacraments of baptism, confirmation, eucharist, and reconciliation. Their use is not limited to adult initiation although they draw their inspiration from the catechumenate. During the time of mystagogia they could be used to help neophytes reflect on those sacraments that have sealed their journey of faith. The order of the sacraments of initiation determines the sequence of the first three panels. A fourth panel—reconciliation—completes the set. The addition of this fourth panel is to provide flexibility for a community which may wish to use them for a group of returning Christians—those seeking to be "remembered" to the community.

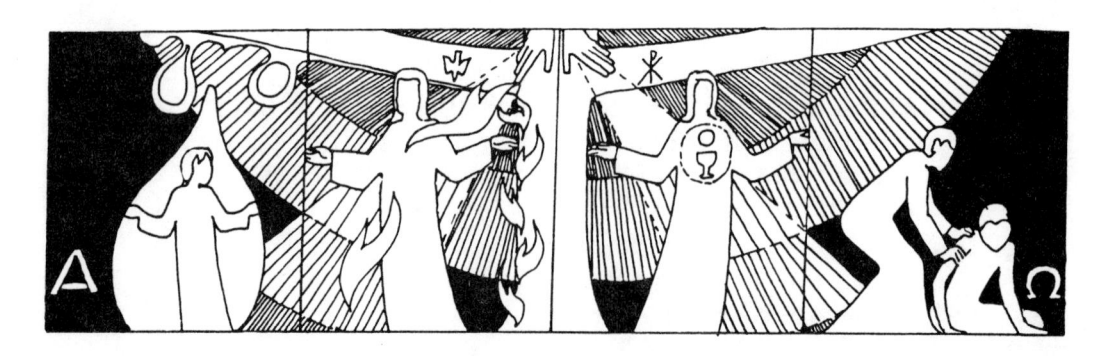

Their use may extend to other occasions, for example, baptism, first communion, reconciliation, confirmation for young Christians. Again they can be used as a visual aid in developing sacramental programs particularly when presenting these programs to parents.

Symbols
The central symbol around which all revolves is the "tree of life," the living cross of Christ. The hands of God are placed at the top center; the dove and the chi-rho are placed on each arm of the cross.

The circle of light behind the tree symbolizes the eternal Father of us all. Rays of light emanate from the hands of the Father connecting all these sacraments.

Panel one—Baptism
The blue, living waters of baptism flow from the tree of life. The blue background symbolizes alpha, our beginning.

Panel two—Confirmation
This panel is red, gold, and white—the colors of the fire of the Spirit; and green—the color of "new life." Flames flow out from the "tree of life."

Panel three—Eucharist
Eucharist, given to us by the risen Lord, is our "food" for the ongoing journey. The colors are white, gold and orange, and the figure is outlined in the green of "new life."

Panel four—Reconciliation
We forgive each other. The colors used are gold, green, white and violet. The background is blue-violet, and symbolized omega, the end that is the beginning.

Green—new life   Violet—repentance   White—neophyte

An Alternative Reconciliation Banner*

This banner has been designed for adult reconciliation liturgies.

On a burgundy or violet backing banner is placed a white circle. This symbolizes the world, and the eternal God.

The chi-rho stands at the top center in red and gold.

We divide ourselves and our world into our light, illuminated side; and our "dark" side. Our light side which responds to the commandment of love, is alive and bright as are those to whom we minister—the "poor" and suffering. They are already filled with the Spirit.

Our dark side becomes blacker when we close our eyes because we turn away from others. There are times when we have to cross the "line" into darkness to become alive ourselves.

The order in which pattern pieces are added.

Add design lines last

This circular motif may be mounted on a rectangular violet backing banner.

*This panel was based on an idea from the chapter "Forgiving" in Albert Nolan's book, *Jesus before Christianity*, Orbis Books, 1978.

The Catechumenate Concludes
After a journey of twelve or more months the catechumenal experience draws to a close at Pentecost.* But the community's responsibility to its new members does not finish. Consideration needs to be given to "after-care" for the new Christian. Thus it is highly recommended that there should be:

Ongoing Formation
Initiation celebrates the beginning of one's faith journey. The years ahead must be seen as opportunities for developing one's knowledge and experience of the Christian faith. There are many avenues through which this can be attained. City dwellers do have more opportunities than those who live in country areas. But even here much is offered in this age of video and cassette tapes.

Days of Prayer
These will provide opportunity for the new Christians to develop their prayer life, and reflect further on the meaning of their initiation experience. *Lex orandi* (the way we pray) is still the touchstone of *lex credendi* (what we believe).

Spiritual Direction
Journeying into the future is never easy. New Christians need that regular reassurance and guidance as they grow in their understanding of what it means to be Christian. There should be no delay in putting new Christians in contact with those skilled in spiritual direction.

Communication
The sense of community that develops during the catechumenate has to be maintained. Continued contact and concern is essential because we are not asked to walk the journey alone.

An Annual Reunion Retreat
This is recommended by the R.C.I.A. It is an important occasion for remembering, sharing, and celebrating. This should not be beyond the resources

---
* See 24. Appendix III, R.C.I.A.

of the average catechumenal community. A suggested outline is included on the following pages.

Annual Retreat—Reunion—Twilight Retreat

Theme
"For all that has been: thanks!
For all that is to come: yes!"
    Dag Hammarskjold

Welcome
Presentation to each of the decorated note book/folder. The jottings that grow out of these sessions may form the basis for future journal memories.

Session 1: Remember Yesterday
Scripture: Abraham (Genesis 12:1-2; 13:14-17)

In my life
- Take time to think back over your journey:
    —recall a moment of hardship or uncertainty;
    —recall a moment of deep joy, peace, a realization.
- What do you believe your God was saying to you?
- Share your reflection with someone in the group.

In the group
- Think back to your first experiences of R.C.I.A. What was in your "baggage" as you set out on this journey (joys, hopes, fears)?
- How have you changed?
- Would you like to thank the group for anything in particular?
- Share in a larger group (4-5 people) or the whole group.

Praying together
- Time of quiet, during which each person writes a note to all others in the group, thanking them for their support, their giftedness along the way. Specially prepared sheets may begin something like this:

As I think back on the journey we have shared together, I would like to thank you for_____
_____
_____
                    (Signed)_____

Play quiet music for the duration. The completed notes, named on the outside, are placed on the central table. Someone serves the group as sorter, another hands the notes to each individual.

Further quiet time, during which the notes are read.

Song "We Gather Together" or "Now Thank We All Our God" (both traditional), or another suitable song. The group joins hands during the singing.

Session 2: Dream About Tomorrow

Song "We Are Companions on the Journey" (Carey Landry) or "We Walk by Faith" (Marty Haugen) or another suitable song.

In my life
As I look to the future
—what are my hopes?
—what are my fears?
—what words of Scripture can I turn to to sustain my belief?
Share this with someone.

In this group
While I know life changes and people must freely move in different directions
—what do I ask of this group?
—what can I offer this group?
Share in a group or the whole group (if possible).

Prayer
Read Jeremiah 29:11
Take time for quiet, then spontaneous reflections/petitions.
then—Father, as I dream about tomorrow, I pray, "Our Father..."
Conclude with the opening hymn.

Session 3: But Live Today
Celebration of Eucharist together.

Preparation
The group divides up to prepare readings, prayers, hymns, banner, altar, etc.

Coming together
Talk over the plans made for this celebration—and some of the reasons why we chose what we did.

Actual celebration
Allow for time and opportunity to share, pray spontaneously and be quiet with our God. The focus "But live today" challenges us to recall the previous sessions but also to celebrate the reality that now is the only precious gift we have from our God.

Suggested Resources List

Catechumenate

Amandolare, Ronald, Thomas P. Ivory and William J. Reedy, eds. *Resource Book for the RCIA*. New York: Sadlier, 1988.

Christian Initiation of Adults: A Commentary (Study Text 10). Washington, D.C.: U.S. Catholic Conference, 1985.

Christian Initiation Resources Reader (Volume IV: Mystagogia and Ministries). New York: Sadlier, 1984.

Duffy, Regis. *On Becoming a Catholic: The Challenge of Christian Initiation*. San Francisco: Harper & Row, 1984.

Duggan, Robert D. *Conversion and the Catechumenate*. New York: Paulist Press, 1984.

Dujarier, M. *The Rites of Christian Initiation*. New York: Sadlier, 1979.

Dunning, James. *New Wine, New Wineskins*. New York: Sadlier, 1981.

Himan, Karen. *Forming a Catechumenate Team*. Chicago: Liturgy Training Publications, 1986.

Johnson, Lawrence J. ed. *Initiation and Conversion*. Collegeville, Minn.: Liturgical Press, 1985.

Lewinski, Ronald. *Welcoming the New Catholic*. Chicago: Liturgy Training Publications, 1983.

Kemp, R. *A Journey in Faith: An Experience of the Catechumenate*. New York: Sadlier, 1979.

McMahon, J. Michael. *Liturgical Commentary: Rite of Christian Initiation of Adults*. Washington, D.C.: FDLC, 1986.

Rite of Christian Initiation of Adults (Study edition). Chicago: Liturgy Training Publications; Washington, D.C.: U.S. Catholic Conference; Collegeville, Minn.: Liturgical Press; New York: Catholic Book Publishing Co., 1988.

Wilde, James A., ed. *A Catechumenate Needs Everybody: Study Guides for Parish Ministers*. Chicago: Liturgy Training Publications, 1988.

_____. *Commentaries on the Rite of Christian Initiation of Adults*. Chicago: Liturgy Training Publications, 1988.

_____. *Parish Catechumenate: Pastors, Presiders, Preachers*. Chicago: Liturgy Training Publications, 1988.

Sacraments

Bausch, William. *A New Look at the Sacraments* (rev.). Mystic, Conn.: Twenty-Third Publications, 1984.

Duffy, Regis. *Real Presence*. San Francisco: Harper & Row, 1982.

Feider, Paul. *The Sacraments: Encountering the Risen Lord*. Notre Dame: Ave Maria Press, 1986.

Hellwig, Monika. *The Meaning of Sacraments*. Dayton: Pflaum Press, 1981.

Martos, Joseph. *Doors to the Sacred*. New York: Doubleday, 1981.

Osborne, Kenan. *The Christian Sacraments of Initiation*. New York: Paulist Press, 1987.

_____. *Sacramental Theology*. New York: Paulist Press, 1988.

Baptism

Huck, Gabe. *Infant Baptism in the Parish*. Chicago: Liturgy Training Publications, 1980.

Kavanagh, Aidan. *The Shape of Baptism: The Rite of Christian Initiation*. New York: Pueblo, 1978.

Keating, Charles. *Welcome to the Christian Community*. VHS Mystic, Conn.: Twenty-Third Publications, 1988. *Bienvenido Sa Usted a la Comunidad Cristiana* (Spanish narration).

Marsh, Thomas. *Gift of Community*. Wilmington: Michael Glazier, 1984.

Mooney, Patrick. *The Baptism of Susan*. VHS Mystic, Conn.: Twenty-Third Publications, 1987.

The Rite of Baptism for Children. Washington, D.C.: U. S. Catholic Conference, 1969.

Searle, Mark. *Christening: The Making of Christians*. Collegeville, Minn.: Liturgical Press, 1980.

Confirmation

Austin, Gerard. *Anointing with the Spirit*. New York: Pueblo, 1985.

Fitzgerald, Timothy. *Confirmation: A Parish Celebration*. Chicago: Liturgy Training Publications, 1983.

Kavanagh, Aidan. *Confirmation: Origins and Reform*. New York: Pueblo, 1988.

Milner, Austin. *The Theology of Confirmation*. Cork, Ireland: Mercier, 1971.

Mooney, Patrick. *Confirmation: Faith Alive*. VHS Mystic, Conn.: Twenty-Third Publications, 1987.

Eucharist

Keifer, Ralph. *Blessed and Broken*. Wilmington: Michael Glazier, 1985.

Lee, Bernard ed. *Alternatives for Worship, Vol. 3, Eucharist*. Collegeville, Minn.: Liturgical Press, 1987.

Mooney, Patrick. *Eucharist: A Gift for Life*. VHS Mystic, Conn.: Twenty-Third Publications, 1987.

Reconciliation

Dallen, James. *The Reconciling Community: The Rite of Penance*. New York: Pueblo, 1986.

Gula, Richard M. *To Walk Together Again*. New York: Paulist Press, 1988.

Lopresti, James. *Penance: Reform Proposal for the Rite*. Washington, D.C.: Pastoral Press, 1987.

Mooney, Patrick. *Penance: Sacrament of Peace*. VHS Mystic, Conn.: Twenty-Third Publications, 1987.

Rite of Penance. New York: Catholic Book Publishing Co., 1975.

The Lectionary

Bausch, William. *Storytelling: Imagination and Faith*. Mystic, Conn.: Twenty-Third Publications, 1984.

_____. *Storytelling: Imagination and Faith*. Audiobook Mystic, Conn.: Twenty-Third Publications, 1987.

Hestenes, Roberta. *Using the Bible in Groups*. Philadelphia: Westminster Press, 1983.

Powell, Karen Hinman and Joseph Sinwell, eds. *Breaking Open the Word of God, Years A, B, and C*. New York: Paulist Press, 1987 and 1988.

Liturgical Year

Adolf, Adam. *The Liturgical Year*. New York: Pueblo, 1981.

Bice-Allen, Thomas. *Lay Ministers in the Eucharistic Community*. VHS Mystic, Conn.: Twenty-Third Publications, 1987.

Johnson, Lawrence J. ed. *The Church Gives Thanks and Remembers*. Collegeville, Minn.: Liturgical Press, 1984.

The Liturgical Year: Celebrating the Mystery of Christ and His Saints (Study Text 9). Washington, D.C.: United States Catholic Conference, 1985.

Symbols

Child, Heather, Dorothy Colles. *Christian Symbols Ancient and Modern*. London: Bell and Hyman, 1979.

Cirlot, J.E. *Dictionary of Symbols, second edition*. London: Routledge and Kegan Paul, 1971.

Environment and Art in Catholic Worship. Washington, D.C.: U. S. Catholic Conference, 1978.

Ferguson, George. *Signs and Symbols in Christian Art*. New York: Oxford University Press, 1981.

Foster, Judy, and Jill Shirvington, O.P. *Share His Glory, Vols. A, B and C*. Melbourne: Collins Dove, 1984.

Horming, Clarence P. *Handbook of Designs and Devices*. New York: Dover Publications, 1959.

Smeets, Renee. *Signs, Symbols and Ornaments*. New York: Van Nostrand and Reinhold Co., 1982.

To Implement Parish Programs...

Celebrating The Fifty Days of Easter
Daniel Connors

Celebrating the Fifty Days of Easter by Daniel Connors offers solid help for sustaining a sense of paschal joy throughout the Easter season by providing a reflection for each of the fifty days. On weekdays, it offers a brief reflection on the liturgical prayers and Scripture (year A, the readings deemed especially appropriate by the RCIA) of the coming Sunday. On the Sundays of the season, it offers a longer reflection on the paschal symbols of baptism, gathering, water, oil, paschal candle, and bread and wine. *Celebrating the Fifty Days of Easter* is for newly baptized adults, RCIA teams, parents helping their children prepare for sacrament, and all members of the church who want to deepen their participation in the mysteries we celebrate.

ISBN: 0-89622-463-5, Paper, 80 pp., $3.95

What others say...

"Connors has a rare gift: he speaks of our prayer, ritual, and tradition in a language most folks can understand. He makes sense of things spiritual and leads us to understand the spirituality of things sensible. Unless you opt to buy a copy for each parishioner, be sure that at least one copy makes it to your library for the spiritual enrichment of those who shape the prayer and ritual of your community's paschaltide."
— AUSTIN FLEMING
Liturgy 90

"Parish clergy, RCIA teams, and DREs should welcome **Celebrating the Fifty Days of Easter**. *This is a clear, concise, usable vehicle to help guide everyone in the parish through the Easter season.*"
— DR. MARY MARGARET SWOGGER, DRE
St. Peter the Apostle Church
Birmingham, Alabama

"Here, at last, is a book that brings home the joy of the church's fifty days of Easter rejoicing! Homilists and all who prepare liturgy will find much food for thought, and recently married couples and new parents will relate especially well to the poignant stories capably told by one who shares the unique experiences of this time of life."
— PAUL COVINO
Liturgical Resource Consultant

"A recommendable resource for the neophyte....Though not explicitly stated I sense an underlying assumption in this author's work: we are called to be sacrament for the world. How right to have something designed for personal reflection be so mission oriented. The best thing about all of this is that the author has created what can be a very fertile ground for reflection without violating or manipulating the Sunday lectionary. Isn't it amazing what can be created when we understand the church's liturgy and allow the lectionary to guide us in unfolding the mysteries we celebrate!"
— REV. RON OAKHAM
Forum
Newsletter of the North American Forum on the Catechumenate

Available from Religious Bookstores or directly from
TWENTY-THIRD PUBLICATIONS • P.O. Box 180, Mystic, CT 06355
1-800-321-0411 • FAX: 1-203-572-0788